SEA KAYAKING

Sea Kayaking

A Manual
for
Long-Distance
Touring

by John Dowd

DOUGLAS & MCINTYRE
VANCOUVER
UNIVERSITY OF WASHINGTON PRESS
SEATTLE

Copyright © 1981, 1983 by John Dowd

REVISED EDITION

DOUGLAS & MCINTYRE LTD.
1615 Venables Street
Vancouver, British Columbia

Canadian Cataloguing in Publication Data

Dowd, John, 1945–
Sea Kayaking

Includes index.
ISBN 0–88894–305–9

1. Canoes and canoeing.   2. Seamanship.
I. Title.
GV783.D69   797.1'22   C81–091064–0

Published simultaneously in the United States of America by the University of Washington Press, Seattle

Library of Congress Cataloging in Publication Data

Dowd, John
Sea Kayaking: a manual for long-distance touring.

Includes index.
1. Sea kayaking—Handbooks, manuals, etc. I. Title.
GV788.5.D68   797.1'22   81–186
ISBN 0–295–95807–3 (University of Washington Press)
AACR1

Photo Credits

CAM BROZE: page 20 (top)
PAUL CAFFYN: page 52
BOB CAIN: page 38
JACQUES DALET: page 212
GEORGE DYSON: pages 21 (bottom), 63 (top)
LEE & JUDY MOYER: pages 6, 21 (top)
WILL NORDBY: pages 14, 20 (bottom)
PETER THOMAS: page 63 (bottom)
CARIBBEAN KAYAK EXPEDITION 1977–8, pages 13 (bottom),
72–73, 84, 120, 136, 162, 186, 198
CHILEAN KAYAK EXPEDITION 1973–4, page 13 (top)

DESIGN
Robert Bringhurst Ltd., Vancouver
COMPOSITION
The Typeworks, Mayne Island, British Columbia
PRINTED & BOUND IN CANADA
by D.W. Friesen & Sons Ltd.

Contents

Acknowledgements

My thanks to Jim Allan, Stephen Besuk, Matt and Cam Broze, Paul Caffyn, Peter Carter, John Chamberlin, Don Cohen, Hilary Collins, John Dawson, George Dyson, Franco Ferrero, Werner Furrer, Chris Furse, Frank Goodman, Cyril Gordon, John Gosling, Paul Grigg, Mark Harrison, Mike Jacques, Peter Johnston, Joe Lamb, Alex Lane, Dr. Hannes Lindemann, Nigel Matthews, Charles Miller, David Raeburn, John Ramwell, Barry Smith, Dieter Stiller, Eric Totty, Phil Walton, for contributing to this book either through their answers to my questions or through their generously offered suggestions and anecdotes. A special thanks to Ken Beard, Stephen Benson, Paul Caffyn, Bob Cain, Jacques Dalet, George Dyson, Judy and Lee Moyer, Will Nordby, Peter Thomas, and Anderson Wilmore for use of their photographs.

For information about the Mariner Self-Rescue, write to Mariner Kayaks, 1005 E. Spruce Street, Seattle, WA 98122.

Finally, I wish to thank my wife Beatrice for helping with the typing and retyping of this book, and my editor, Robert Bringhurst. I shudder to think what it would have been like without their assistance.

J.D.

NOTE ON TERMINOLOGY

In this book the words "kayak" and "canoe" are interchangeable synonyms. British and American usage of the words at present differs confusingly, but this confusion cannot endure forever. The boats themselves, and the love of them, are increasingly widespread. Those who call themselves kayakers and those who, meaning the same thing, call themselves canoeists, must sooner or later tire of mutual misunderstanding. I use both words, but always with one meaning. At no point in this book do I discuss the merits of the open or Canadian canoe. I speak only of those decked and skirted craft, evidently of Arctic origin, for which the traditional Inuit name is *kayak*.

Introduction

For as long as I have been reading books about kayaking, I have been distressed to find sea kayaking usually squeezed into one chapter somewhere near the back. Yet the kayak was conceived and first built for the sea. Canoeing books even assume, as a rule, that one would never consider paddling more than a few miles from shore but in fact many inspiring sea voyages have been made by kayak since John MacGregor first launched his clinker-built *Rob Roy* in 1865. Adventurers such as Frederic Fenger, Karl Schott, Gino Watkins, Franz Romer, Hannes Lindemann and others have travelled many of the world's coastlines and island chains, and some of them have crossed great oceans by kayak.

In recent years, dogma evolved by a generation of canoeists weaned on slalom canoeing, whitewater and long distance racing has been fruitlessly misapplied to the sea. The old knowledge – which was to a large extent lost – is only now being relearned. I would like to think that my own experiences on the sea have taught me most of the basic lessons, yet I have a nagging suspicion that in twenty years' time I will laugh at such a notion. I tell myself that it has been an advantage for me to learn most of what I know from my own mistakes, free of the strictures of so-called right and wrong ways, which I have since discovered have little to do with the realities of sea canoeing. In canoeing as in other pursuits, people eager for fixed answers have sometimes enshrined as dogma the tentative suggestions of others who were guessing beyond their experience. Some of the supposedly tried and true methods of kayak rescue, to take an important example, have not really been tried at all by their exponents except in sheltered waters, and are perfectly hopeless under real conditions. Yet men have crossed the Atlantic alone in kayaks, capsizing in violent storms and battered by outrageous waves, and have rescued themselves by methods whose usefulness is thereby proven. The methods of rescue and self-rescue I describe in this book are methods I have inadvertently tested on several occasions and which I am still alive to refine. I have had some chance also to test the schoolbook group-rescue techniques, and I can testify all too grimly to the ease with which they fail.

I too have had to guess beyond my experience on occasion during the writing of this book, but I have tried to make it clear when I am guessing. I am no expert, for instance, on the usefulness of the Eskimo roll as a routine for handling ocean breakers. My personal preference at sea is a stable kayak which braces well and in which the roll is more a stunt than a reliable solution. Sailing, sport surf canoeing and the study of sea ice are also activities in which my experience is limited, and where these topics have arisen in relation to sea kayak touring, I have drawn to some extent on the experience of others.

The late 1970s saw a remarkable increase in the number of ambitious sea kayaking expeditions. Once the prerogative of a few maverick individuals, sea kayaking has been taken up by club canoeists – particularly on the west coast of North America and in Britain. A new wave of enthusiasm, triggered and encouraged to some extent by commercial interests and their well-publicized demonstration expeditions, has taken hold. For example, Frank Goodman has established a worldwide organization of sea canoeists to spread the faith and sell his Nordkapps, while Derek Hutchinson, author of *Sea Canoeing,* is noted for his three designs, the Baidarka, Umnak and Icefloe. John Ramwell, who wrote *Sea Touring,* the only other book on the subject, organizes an annual Sea Symposium and runs an Advanced Sea Canoeing Club com-

plete with neckties and pins. With less fanfare, members of
the Washington Kayak Club have been exploring the rugged
British Columbia and Alaska coast in steadily increasing
numbers for two decades. The kayak, I believe, is making its
way back to the sea where it was born and where it belongs.

During the preparation of this book I corresponded with
many other sea canoeists, peppering them with questions
about the nature and extent of their experiences, their knowledge and their thoughts on the subject. I am grateful for the
answers I received, many of which have found their way into
the text. I am also certain there are many others who have
made magnificent trips and have been so quiet about it that I
had no access to the knowledge they hold. It is in the nature of
the fraternity that in most coastal cities one can meet more
dedicated sea kayakers by watching seaways and automobile
roof racks than by contact with the numerous clubs.

Sea boats are often designed and manufactured as surrepti-
tiously as they are paddled – and this too is in the long-
standing arctic tradition. Recently, however, several well-
designed and mass-produced fibreglass kayaks have appeared
on the market. There is now, as there was long ago, a kayak
for almost every purpose – from the slender West Greenland
style boat, originally designed for hunting among ice floes,
to the 40–foot baidarka which can carry six paddlers plus a
dog team and half a ton of supplies down the length of the
Aleutians. Most of the boats in use these days, however, are
singles (one-man kayaks) or cruising doubles. Each has its own
merits and limitations, and each has its band of single-minded
adherents. There are many designs, but each is a sea kayak: a
silent, responsive craft, with clean lines and one of the most
basic forms of propulsion there is: a boat which impels the
lone paddler into reverent harmony with the sea and enables
the explorer to probe where no other vessel can reach, so silent
the photographer or hunter can slip up to wild animals with-

out ever disturbing them, and so rugged and indomitable it can ride out gales on the open sea.

Because the knowledge required for sea kayaking is so encompassing, I have frequently chosen to omit the basic in favour of the specific. For example, the chapter on first aid neglects such essentials as rescue breathing and treatment of bleeding, since these are well covered in general publications on first aid. My chapter concentrates instead on canoe-related ailments. I trust the reader will already know the basics – for know them he must, if he is embarking on an expedition.

Navigation, camping and general survival are other areas in which I assume the reader is not a novice. The information presented here is geared to kayaking situations and seen from the viewpoint of a kayaker. Assuming that most problems encountered on a day or week-end cruise will occur on an expedition-size trip, but not vice-versa, I have tended to conc entrate upon the problems of long kayak journeys. The emphasis upon open water crossings is based on a similar assumption that the required knowledge fully encompasses a knowledge of coastal cruising.

I have attempted to make this a book for the adventurous sea kayaker, novice and expert alike. It is my feeling that a sea kayak expedition can be the ultimate kayaking experience, and I will be happy if this guide makes it safer and more accessible for those who share that view, or who simply would like to see for themselves.

Above: Laguna San Rafael, Chile. Below: Maracas beach, Trinidad

Parafoil kites may be used for off-the-wind sailing.

I
Equipment

THE BOAT

Sea kayaks or sea canoes are distinguished from river kayaks by a multitude of features for which we have one word: seaworthiness. A sea boat may or may not roll easily, but it must slice through or ride over waves of all sizes, track dependably regardless of the direction of the sea, respond to the paddle, carry your gear, and stand up to continuous punishment from wave action, weather, sand, rocky beaches, sea ice, and sometimes very large, very inquisitive fish.

That said, there are still boats of many sorts to choose from, and every dedicated canoeist is his own best authority on "the best kayak." What you have to do is choose the right one for your use. There are countless manufacturers, most of them very small operations, and design is by no means stagnant. Nevertheless, the choice at present comes down to three readily available types of boat:

1 The sporty kayaks (West Greenland types)
2 The cruising singles (King Island types)
3 The cruising doubles (Aleut baidarka types)

Most sea boats have a sharp prow and an angular or even knife-like forefoot. Amidships, the hull is often rounded and flattened in cross section. Farther aft, the cross section resumes its rounded V shape, and the stern itself may be as sharp as the prow. As a rule, sea canoes have little rocker (the curvature upward of the keel-line towards stem and stern as the boat is viewed in profile.) A deep, sharp stem and stern allow the boat to track through the waves without yawing under the alternating thrust of the paddle. The rounded section amidships allows the boat to slide in breakers, and the partial flattening under the cockpit increases stability. A high prow is found in some designs, including many of the surviving or recorded Eskimo and Aleut boats, a useful feature in ice but of questionable value in open water. In some hulls you will also see chines. These are ridges, angular in cross section, running lengthwise along the hull between gunwale and keel. In fabric or skin-covered boats they are caused by the tension of the skin across a framing rib; a similar feature is sometimes moulded into fibreglass boats. (The Anas Acuta, Mariner and Escape are examples of this. With the Mariner and Escape, the chine aids turning when the boat is leaned to one side.)

Slalom kayaks, designed for quick turns in rivers rather than tracking at sea, have much more rocker than a sea boat, and their hulls are generally flatter in cross section amidships and considerably rounder at bow and stern. A high-volume river boat is often used for surf canoeing and when fitted with a skeg or rudder will sometimes serve for a short sea voyage, but the compromise is not finally a happy one. Away from whitewater, it is better to have a kayak true to the ancestry of the craft: a boat designed specifically for the sea.

The West Greenland Kayak

These single seater kayaks are usually between 17 and 21 feet long with an 18-inch to 23-inch beam. Commonly they have a rounded hull, hard chine or moderate V hull with very little rocker. Essentially they are coastal and protected-water craft, and a paddler using them in wind or open water must be comfortable with his rolling technique. These boats depend upon the skill of the paddler for their seaworthiness. They are too small and too tippy to allow sleep during illness or long crossings.

The West Greenland originals were made from sealskin with a fragile wood and bone frame, but today the best boats in this style are fibreglass. A well-known version is the Nordkapp, produced by Valley Canoe Products in England. Although this 21-inch beam kayak has been used on some impressive trips (most notably the circumnavigation of New Zealand, Britain and Australia by Paul Caffyn), it is nevertheless best suited for day-tripping. It is a boat for those with a passion for technique, style or both. Its awkward storage, cramped cockpit and wet ride render it less practical for touring than its North American equivalents, the Mariner and Heron, designed respectively by Matt and Cam Broze of Mariner Kayaks and Tom Derrer of Eddyline.

Derek Hutchinson, long time proponent of narrow boats and designer of the 20-inch Baidarka Explorer, has recently shifted to beamier touring kayaks with his Icefloe though, as with so many British-designed sea kayaks, the preoccupation with "Eskimo looks" has resulted in the absurdity of kayaks with lines designed for negotiating sea ice being extolled for virtues they do not have as sea boats.

Both the Nordkapp and the several Hutchinson designs are equipped with bulkheads and hatches fore and aft, providing buoyancy and dry stowage. Because the hatches are so small, however, they are more difficult to load and unload than a conventional hardshell kayak, in which gear must be bagged and slid fore and aft from the cockpit.

The Mariner and Heron, although also suffering the inconvenience of small hatches, both provide through-the-cockpit loading for the equivalent of a large backpack of gear. Tom Derrer's Sandpiper, which has a 23-inch beam, is fitted with a more useful 17 inch by 12 inch hatch.

The great advantages of West Greenland type kayaks are the ease with which they can be rolled, and their generally higher top speed. Most, however, would be improved by the addition of a good rudder. The most obvious disadvantage of these boats is limited stowage space, rendering them unsuitable for any expedition on which food and equipment must be carried in quantity. Their more serious drawback, however, is that they are neither stable enough nor roomy enough for real relaxation, or even to serve as a platform for photography. They are deadly if their occupant becomes exhausted or incapacitated at sea in severe conditions.

The Single Cruising Kayak

This plump cousin to the Greenland-type kayak was especially popular between the 1930s and 1960s. It is usually shorter than the Greenland boat – between 14 and 17 feet – with a beam of about 24 to 30 inches, often with a chined hull. Some, such as the Folbot, have a grand 32-inch beam and you can stand up in them. These old-style singles often have an enlarged cockpit with an oversize spray deck, which makes loading and unloading easier but leaves the boat more vulnerable to the force of breaking waves. Spray decks, however, *can* be reinforced, and touring boats usually have so much equipment aboard that the spray deck gains support from tightly packed gear. The stability of these boats enables you to rest and relax in them, so they can be safely included on journeys with prolonged exposure to open sea. They have a greater load-carrying capacity than the sporty kayaks and, though their generally higher profile makes them vulnerable to wind, they tend to give a drier ride. The beamier singles are usually about ½ knot slower than the West Greenland boats and are more difficult to roll, but then they are far less likely to require rolling.

Future designs for single sea kayaks will probably reflect a return to these beamier boats, after the sea limits of the narrower Greenland kayaks have been reached and interest in longer ocean-going trips increases. Lee Moyer, for example, of Pacific Water Sports in Seattle, has developed the 16-foot Sea Otter, a fibreglass sea kayak with a 25½-inch beam and an aft compartment with a large hatch for easy loading. The boat is designed for cruising the rugged British Columbia and Alaska coast. It is stable and will carry a substantial load. Another contemporary single cruising design is the Orca, a 17-footer introduced by Eddyline. The Broze brothers have come up with the Escape, and Nimbus with the Seafarer.

The immediate ancestor of the hardshell cruising single is the collapsible or foldboat – a design pioneered in Germany early in this century, and itself based on originals from the Canadian Arctic. The German models were originally manufactured for lakes and rivers. They have long since lost their pre-eminence in this latter field to hardshell kayaks of fibreglass and Kevlar, but the suitability of some of these collapsibles for use on the open sea has given them a whole new purpose. (In fact the English Channel was crossed in a German-made folding kayak as early as 1909.)

The Double or Triple Cruising Kayak

Whereas the Eskimos of West Greenland developed their kayaks for inshore hunting, the Aleuts of Alaska designed their larger models for longer, more exposed voyages. These boats, which the Russians called baidarka, were further enlarged at the instigation of the Russian fur traders and used for hunting and trading voyages east and south from the Aleutians as far as the coast of California. Often over 30 feet in length, they were paddled by as many as six men. These Russian-Aleut hybrids

19

The Brozes' Mariner is swift and narrow but still built to carry a load while Werner Furrer's roomy WK2.560 is the Pacific coast freighter.

When is a kayak not a kayak? Above is a 16–foot single cruising kayak (a Sea Otter), and below is George Dyson's 45–foot, six-man, three-masted *Mount Fairweather*, with detachable outriggers and weatherproof Perspex domes.

varied greatly in design but remained at least loosely based on the original Aleut craft. The closest approximations today are the baidarkas built by George Dyson of Vancouver, B. C., whose book on Aleutian kayaks is eagerly awaited. Using modern materials – chiefly fibreglass and aluminum – Dyson has built several kayaks with many of the original baidarka features. His triple seater is 28 feet long with a 30-inch beam. It is very stable and can carry a sail. Dyson's sail design is most original; ashore it can double as a tent. Like its predecessors, this baidarka can also carry a fine load (600 lbs) of equipment. It has a sturdy rudder and is very seaworthy.

With the exception of a three-place Sisiutl, the commercial market is at present limited to doubles, either hardshell fibreglass or folding boats of rubberized fabric with collapsible wood frames. There are many manufacturers, large and small, of hardshell doubles, including Pacific Water Sports in the United States, P&H Fibreglass in the U.K., Klepper and Lettmann in West German, and Frontiersman in Canada. Folding doubles are made by Folbot in the United States, Pouch in East Germany, Klepper in West Germany, Nautiraid in France, Feathercraft in Canada, and by several other firms.

CHOOSING A KAYAK

There are something like 40 different models of sea kayak manufactured in the Pacific Northwest alone and choosing the right boat can be difficult. For a start, you should always insist on paddling any kayak before you buy it. Even if you have little previous kayak experience, you will know at once if it fits you. Although it is probably true that you can get used to almost anything, your impressions as a novice are usually dependable. There are, however, certain criteria which will immediately reduce your choice from 40 to 2 or 3 kayaks.

Choose a two-seater if:

a) one paddler is significantly stronger than the other or if you intend carrying children;

b) you need a double to add safety to group travel;

c) you plan a particularly arduous or risky trip.

Choose a single-seater if:

a) you wish to paddle alone most of the time;

b) you and your partner are independent types of similar paddling strength and ability.

If your choice is a single, you must then decide among about a dozen or more models. Fantasize about what you would like to do with your kayak. Bear in mind that generally your dependence upon technique decreases as the beam of the boat increases. If you like honing your technique and going fast on the sea, look to the narrower, tippier boats. If you are mostly out there for the wilderness or sea experiences with a pile of camping gear, you may prefer a more stable craft. The most popular North American boats are around 25 inches in the beam; the most popular British ones are around 21 inches.

Next, look at your special requirements. Do you need to carry a lot of gear? Which boat has the most efficient loading system? Which has a seat that suits your shape? If you are a wildlife photographer, look for a boat with a rudder; it will improve your ability to control your approach to animals. If you plan on parafoil sailing, the rudder is a big advantage. Above all, look for a boat that looks nice and feels nice to you. Weight is important, and a boat built from Kevlar can weigh in at around 30 lbs; the same boat in fibreglass would be 40–45 lbs.

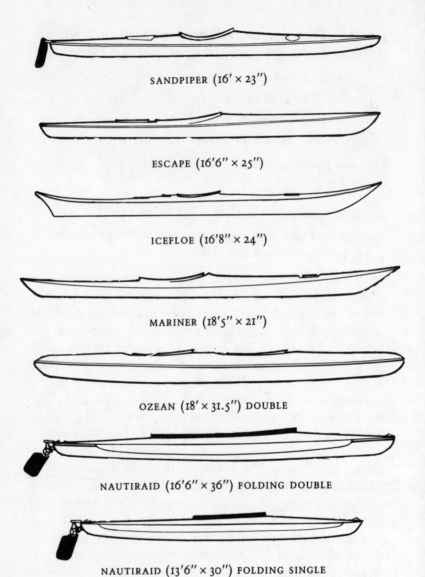

SANDPIPER (16′ × 23″)

ESCAPE (16′6″ × 25″)

ICEFLOE (16′8″ × 24″)

MARINER (18′5″ × 21″)

OZEAN (18′ × 31.5″) DOUBLE

NAUTIRAID (16′6″ × 36″) FOLDING DOUBLE

NAUTIRAID (13′6″ × 30″) FOLDING SINGLE

FIG. I.I SOME OF THE MANY KAYAKS NOW ON THE MARKET.

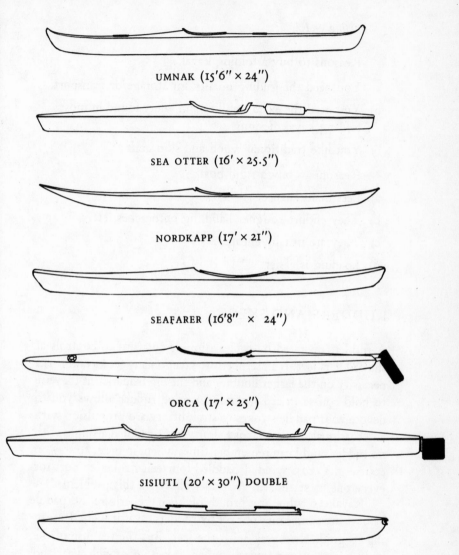

UMNAK (15'6" × 24")

SEA OTTER (16' × 25.5")

NORDKAPP (17' × 21")

SEAFARER (16'8" × 24")

ORCA (17' × 25")

SISIUTL (20' × 30") DOUBLE

KLEPPER AERIUS II (17' × 35") FOLDING DOUBLE

DIMENSIONS GIVEN ARE LENGTH OVERALL AND BEAM.

Folding or Rigid?

Reasons to buy a folding kayak:

a) You need the folding quality for storage or transport.

b) You need the extra stability and safety found in most folding kayak designs.

c) You like traditional wood and skin craft.

Reasons to buy a rigid boat:

a) Less maintenance.

b) They endure rougher handling on beaches, etc.

c) They are usually cheaper.

d) Loading is easier.

RUDDERS AND SKEGS

A rudder, operated by cables running forward to controls at the paddlers feet, is a useful effort-saver on any sea kayak. It is a necessity on the larger doubles and the big baidarkas if they are to hold course in cross winds. A good rudder allows you to devote your paddle strokes to straightforward propulsion with an occasional support stroke. For years I paddled a single with no rudder, and I can remember times when, in order to stay on course in a cross wind, I paddled fourteen strokes to port for every one to starboard. A rudder alleviates this problem.

Kayakers who are proud of their repertoire of paddle strokes are sometimes put off by rudders, as if it were demeaning to guide the kayak with the feet. But the real use of the rudder is on a long voyage, where it can save much wear and tear on belly and shoulder muscles. A well-designed rudder can always be cocked out of the water for intricate manoeuvring

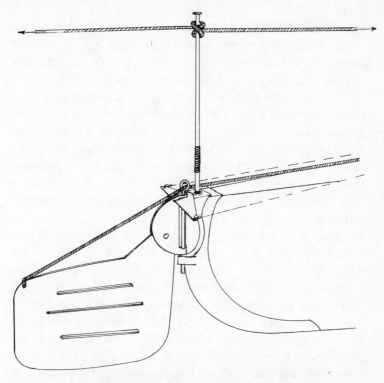

FIG. I.2   A GOOD TOURING SINGLE CAN BE PADDLED WITHOUT A
RUDDER, BUT A RUDDER SAVES EFFORT, PARTICULARLY IN CROSS
WINDS. ALL DOUBLES SHOULD BE FITTED WITH RUDDERS. THE
ILLUSTRATION SHOWS A TOWING LINE PASSING ABOVE THE
RUDDER ASSEMBLY, AND A FLEXIBLE POST TO PREVENT FOULING.

when the fancy paddling may really be required. Probably the
best combination is to have a sea kayak which paddles well
without a rudder but has one anyway.

In doubles, rudder controls can be in either the forward
(No. 1) or aft (No. 2) cockpit. The paddler in the No. 1 cockpit
has an unobstructed view of the bow and what lies immedi-

ately ahead, while the person in the No. 2 position has a more commanding view of the whole boat and a greater sense of control. It is useful to fit auxiliary stirrups to the rudder cables so they can be operated from either cockpit.

Rudders take quite a hammering on a long trip so they must be strongly built. They should be cocked with a string or a paddle for negotiating surf or for lying to a drogue, and should cock automatically on striking a submerged rock. The rudder assembly frequently becomes fouled when towing, though this can be avoided by running the tow line through a short, flexible whip above the rudder and taking up the weight carefully.

A skeg, to a kayaker, is simply a rudder than cannot be turned. It differs from a rudder in the same way deodorant differs from perfume, i.e. it corrects defective hull function whereas the rudder enhances that function. The skeg will, in effect, shift the pivot point to the rear of the boat, making the boat far more directional. Skegs should be designed so that the paddler can remove them while seated in the boat, before approaching a beach through surf or when lying to a drogue. New Zealander Paul Caffyn's homemade skeg, for example, is cocked automatically by a length of shock cord when a line from the cockpit is released. Paul fitted a deep rudder to his boat for his Australian circumnavigation.

PADDLES

Paddles are such personal items that you must take special care with their selection. The ideal length is generally considered to be a little beyond the distance from the flat of your feet to your outstretched fingertips, but the preferences of experienced paddlers of my acquaintance vary so greatly that this rule means

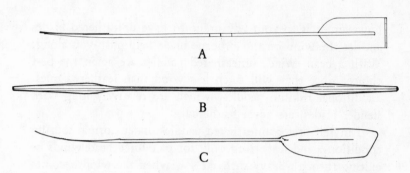

FIG. 1.3 (A) A STANDARD COLLAPSIBLE TOURING PADDLE: (B) THE
QUILL, AN ESKIMO-TYPE TOURING PADDLE BY TRUE NORTH
PADDLE CO: (C) AN ASYMETRICAL TOURING PADDLE

little. Wider boats, however, generally suit longer paddles
than narrow boats. The shafts must be strong, oval and well
cared for to avoid damaging your hands. Most sea canoeists
preferred wooden paddles until recently, when Lendal of
Scotland, as well as Eddyline and Werner Furrer Jr. in Seattle,
began producing good fibreglass cruising paddles.

Large paddle blades move more water and require more
muscle than small blades, and short paddles demand a faster
stroke than long ones. Asymetric blades reduce twisting of
the paddle shaft in your hands. Avoid slalom and racing paddles, which are short with large spoons, since they combine
the features a sea kayaker is likely to want least. If you have a
double kayak, be sure that both paddles have the same length,
otherwise you will have difficulty synchronizing your stroke.

If you have a collapsible paddle, you will be able to vary the
relative angles of the blades to suit conditions. When the
blades are at right angles to each other they are said to be fully
feathered, and when the blades are in one plane they are said to
be unfeathered. Feathering reduces windage on the airborne
blade when travelling into the wind. With a following wind,

however, it is to your advantage to have unfeathered blades and let the wind on the airborne blade help push you along. With a beam wind, unfeathered paddles are again the best choice, since they will catch less wind than feathered ones. Traditional Eskimo paddles, which are relatively long with slender blades, are never feathered.

I myself prefer unfeathered paddles under normal touring conditions, and feathering only for gale-force head winds or exiting through heavy surf. At sea, when the wind becomes too strong to paddle easily, unfeathered paddles are less likely to go spinning out of your hands as the wind catches first one angle and then the other. They are also less likely to catch a sideways gust and face you with the option of hanging onto your paddle and capsizing or letting go one end of the shaft and losing your stroke. If you have agile wrists, you will be able to retain your grip on the shaft and retrieve the paddle from the sea. If not, you won't have to worry about the angle of your paddle – you won't have one! Another problem with feathered paddles is that over long periods they increase the chance of canoeist's arm and tenosynovitis, which result from the twisting motion feathered paddles require. In fact, in view of their few advantages and serious disadvantages, I find it a wonder feathered paddles ever became popular, much less entrenched as they are in modern sea canoeing dogma.

SPRAY SKIRTS AND SPRAY DECKS

A spray skirt is a skirt of neoprene or elastic-fringed nylon designed to prevent water entering the boat through the cockpit. The smaller the cockpit, the less expansive the skirt and the smaller the chance of the surf pushing it in. A large cockpit, on the other hand, is more convenient for entry and makes for easier loading and greater general comfort in the boat. On a full day's trip such comfort is not just a luxury, it becomes a necessity. You have to strike a balance between safety and convenience. If the spray skirt is fitted with a sturdy zipper which slides from chest almost to the deck, you can enter and leave the boat without removing the spray skirt – but even more important when the seas are very rough, a zipper gives quick access to your gear without your having to take off the spray skirt. It enables you to close the cockpit the instant you see an approaching whitecap. A spray skirt can be difficult to put on the cockpit at sea, especially if your hands are cold, so it is good to be able to put it on the boat and leave it there. Once you have a zipper sewn into your spray skirt, you will wonder how you ever got along without one. (You may also find it hard to remember what it was like paddling with a dry crotch, unless you have a waterproof zipper.)

A sturdy "panic loop" at the front of the spray skirt makes it easier to remove. The spray skirt should be attached loosely enough to be removed by a pull at this loop yet tightly enough to withstand the pounding of a breaker. Shoulder straps can prevent the skirt riding down on your body and enable you to empty the pools from the skirt with a shrug. A useful variation is the anorak which fits around the cockpit over the top of the spray skirt or, like the old Eskimo model, attaches directly to the cockpit, becoming a combination spray skirt and jacket. The anorak too may be fitted with a zipper enabling access to the interior.

Spray decks, found on many of the old style cruising boats, are watertight covers for the enlarged cockpits. Because of their large area, it is important that these be securely attached to the coaming of the boat. Turnbuckles are suitable for this purpose, but should ideally be combined with a further waterproofing system such as a tuck-in flap to prevent waves forcing water beneath the cover. Expansive spray decks for single-cockpit doubles should be reinforced with a plywood frame between the cockpits to give added protection against breaking waves and to prevent formation of the annoying little pool of water which will otherwise gather between the paddlers. The plywood also gives the rear paddler a useful working surface for map-reading, meals or the like.

RIGGING

There is no one way to lay out the deck of a kayak. Some people like the deck crisscrossed with nylon webbing and shock cord; others (myself included) prefer it clean. Certain features are necessary, however. A sea-going kayak should have secure loops at either end, to which are attached 10-foot bow and stern painters. These are normally tied off to cleats each side of the cockpit(s). I also use four small cleats to attach the map case, and a variety of sturdier cleats to take the shroud, stays and sheets when sailing. When canoeing open water or lee shores, I rig a 120-foot running line through the bow loop ready to take a drogue or regular anchor. Spare paddles and other equipment are sometimes secured beneath the deck webbing, but it is safer to make special pouches for essential items and use the webbing for more casual storage – or for holding onto the boat after a capsize.

SEATS

A host of experiments have been tried by sore paddlers – from custom-built moulded fibreglass seats to wheelchair seats and inflated wheelbarrow tubes. Many solutions can claim some success, but there is no real answer to the discomfort of staying seated in your kayak for two, twelve, or twenty hours at a time. Backrests, which are frowned upon by river canoeists, are a great asset to the long-distance paddler. Whether you paddle or rest, the support of a backrest is invaluable – even if this simply consists of a strategically placed piece of baggage.

To economize on space I have taken to sitting on my wet-suit and deflated air mattress, both articles I may want close at hand in an emergency. It is, however, useful if your seat allows seawater to drain away so you won't be sitting all day in a puddle.

BUOYANCY SYSTEMS

Without special buoyancy systems, most boats will sink as soon as they fill with water. The best place for buoyancy is along the gunwales, where it offers stability when the boat is awash. When placed at either end, flotation chambers occupy valuable storage space and create an axis around which a flooded boat can spin, thus making it tricky to re-enter without overbalancing again. Buoyancy may be provided by inflatable air sacks, flotation material such as polystyrene, chambers with watertight bulkheads, or a watertight sea sock fitted to the cockpit. Additional flotation is created by carrying clothing, sleeping bags and other light items in sealed waterproof bags.

Watertight bulkheads provide dry stowage and buoyancy at the same time, and they reduce the volume of water you have to pump or bail from a flooded cockpit, but there are disquieting reports of their flooding and the paddler's being unable to pump them dry. In theory, of course, this should not happen, but several sea canoeists have told me unpleasant stories of flooding compartments. Paul Caffyn, for example, describes a time when the after compartment of his Nordkapp flooded, leaving him to go in through heavy surf with the bow riding high in the air. Apparently his boat surfed remarkably well in that posture, but in the open sea such a mishap could prove disastrous. Placing one-way valves in the bilge between the cockpit and the compartments would be an easier solution than fitting three pumps. Water could then flow through the bulkheads into the cockpit where it could be reached with the regular bilge pump. But such a valve is yet one more thing that can malfunction.

If you choose a cruising kayak with watertight bulkheads, check that there is leg room enough to wriggle down for a rest. This ability to stretch out can make a great difference to your comfort on a long crossing.

THE COCKPIT SOCK

The cockpit sock is one more bag for the last baggable item, the paddler himself. Although available in Europe for a number of years, North Americans have only had access to it since 1980. The sock is a waterproof bag, set into the cockpit after the boat is loaded, and attached by its elastic rim to the coaming – just like the spray skirt which fits right on top of it. The paddler sits in the sock. If he fails to roll and is forced to bail out, only the sock fills with water. All the while it remains attached to the coaming, protecting the gear inside and guaranteeing the buoyancy of the boat. Rudder controls can be operated readily through the sock. During trials with two socks fitted to a Sisiutl, we were able to re-enter *and* resume normal paddling within one minute. Fears of entanglement expressed by some appear to be unfounded and not dissimilar to

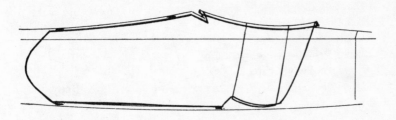

FIG. I.4 A COCKPIT SOCK OF PROOFED NYLON MAKES IT EASY
TO DRAIN THE BOAT IN THE EVENT OF A CAPSIZE.

early arguments against the use of sprayskirts. It has not
proved necessary to invert the socks, which in modern fibreglass kayaks are held in place by a strong vacuum.

DROGUE, SEA-CHUTE AND ANCHOR

A drogue (sea anchor) is a necessary item on any journey with
open sea to leeward; this includes inter-island passages and
coastal kayaking with prevailing offshore winds. Its main
function is to reduce wind drift at sea, but I have heard of its
being used to stabilize entry through surf. It pays to keep the
drogue ready for instant use, the bitter end attached to a
strong point on the boat such as a bridle around the coaming.
It can then be led through a loop at the bow and back to the
'tween deck or after-deck, where it is folded and held in place
by shock cord. The drogue is attached to the boat by approximately 120 feet of nylon parachute cord which, when not in
use, is carefully coiled and tied to prevent tangles, and then
tucked inside the folded canopy.

The best material for standard sea anchors seems to be rip-

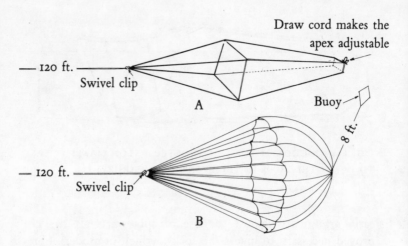

FIG I.5   (A) A DROGUE, AND (B) A SEA-CHUTE. THE MOUTH OF
THE DROGUE SHOULD BE ABOUT 18″ TO 24″ DIAMETER, WHILE
THE DIAMETER OF THE SEA-CHUTE MIGHT BE 4′ OR 5′.

stop nylon or similar fabric which is lightweight and will not
rot if it is stored damp. For a loaded double, an effective size is
36 inches long with an entrance 20 inches square and an apex
aperture about 4 inches square. A swivel at the junction of
the line and the drogue traces will reduce the tendency to
tangle. Most drogues designed for yachts have a trip-line
attached to their apex, but for use with a kayak this is not
necessary. If the drogue becomes too heavy to retrieve, you
need only paddle a little to ease the tension on the line.

A sea-chute is a larger alternative to the sea anchor and is
built exactly like a regular parachute. It is more effective at
stopping wind drift and indeed it can be so effective as to cause
considerable stress in a big sea. With a large sea-chute (5 to 6
feet in diameter), it is important to have a full length of nylon
cable so there is plenty of stretch to absorb the shock. It is also
advisable to attach a float to the crown of the chute by a

10–foot line. This prevents the chute from sinking too deep and holding you down into a wave.

A bottom anchor is hardly standard equipment for most kayaks, but it can be useful if you should choose to sleep in your boat near shore – either because you are unable to land or because for some reason the land is too inhospitable. A small Danforth or Bruce anchor with about 15 feet of chain is suitable. It can be attached to the already rigged sea anchor warp. The anchor comes in handy if you plan to fish or dive from the canoe. George Dyson frequently anchors his big baidarkas offshore to avoid the hassle of dragging them out of the way of the tide, or to avoid the mosquitoes and blackflies ashore.

SAFETY EQUIPMENT

I list here a good deal of safety equipment. To carry it all would be ludicrous, but each article has its use. Just assess the problems you are likely to encounter and take what you are most likely to need.

Pumps & Bailers

Ideally, a well-found sea kayak needs two bilge pumps: a foot-operated, low-volume pump and a hand-operated, higher-capacity pump. This may sound a little excessive to people with utterly dry glass boats, but as a folding boat enthusiast, I consider both pumps among the most important pieces of my safety equipment. Each pump has its own function.

The foot pump, with a capacity of about one gallon per minute, should be mounted to one side of the rudder controls with its intake at the lowest point of the boat. Its purpose is to keep pace with the seepage from waves washing over the boat or from small hull leaks. It comes into its own during rough conditions when you are taking seas frequently or when for some other reason it is unsafe to pause and bail. This is the case with a strong wind on a dangerous lee shore or in a gale-force head wind. Without the foot pump, your boat fills gradually and becomes less stable. You must bail, yet you cannot afford to stop paddling. You do not have to be on a thousand-mile journey to find yourself in this situation; you can encounter such conditions on any day trip. The most common use of the little foot pump, however, is to pump the bilges routinely with a minimum of fuss and no break in the paddling rhythm.

With a capacity of perhaps 12 gallons per minute, the hand pump is your pump for emergencies. It too can be used to drain off routine seepage, but you must stop paddling to do so. Depending on the model, it can be operated through the unzipped spray skirt, mounted semi-permanently through the deck behind the rear cockpit, or stored inside, then taken out and attached to a permanently placed hose with an outlet beside the cockpit. The main emergency use for this pump is to drain the kayak after a capsize.

Other bailing devices may include your toilet-pot, which we trust will have a generous capacity and can help if you capsize in calm waters. A sponge will afford you the luxury of reaching the last drops.

Life Jacket or Personal Flotation Device (PFD)

Obviously a non-swimmer would be foolish to go kayaking without a life jacket, but those who go down to the sea in canoes should know how to swim. For a good swimmer, the chief value of a life jacket is that it will save him from having

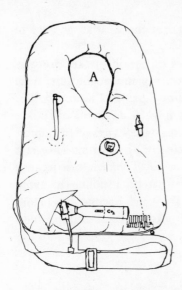

FIG. 1.6 (A) THE INFLATABLE MAE WEST LIFE JACKET, AND (B) A
FLOTATION VEST, BETTER SUITED TO WHITEWATER KAYAKING
THAN TO OCEAN TOURING

to swim: it will allow him to hold himself hunched in the fetal
position and so almost double the time he can survive in cold
water.

Of the many life jackets and buoyancy aids on the market,
I prefer the old Mae West variety, often still to be found on
commercial aircraft. Whether stowed or worn, these can be
kept totally deflated and out of the way until needed, and then
inflated instantly by CO_2 cartridge or patiently by mouth.
Unfortunately, not all models have coast guard approval. The
best are fitted with an automatic salt-cell light and sometimes
a sack of marker dye. They should also carry a plastic whistle.
Deflated, they are comfortable to paddle in and they fold away
into a compact parcel about the size of a lunch box. Next best,
in my view, are the non-inflatable kayakers' life vests, which

offer a measure of protection against the weather and are of moderate bulk.

Many of the traditional roles of the life jacket are performed more efficiently by a wetsuit or immersion suit, since these provide increased protection against the real killer, which is hypothermia, not drowning. A deflatable life jacket can be worn handily in conjunction with a wetsuit or immersion suit, and you can swim efficiently by deflating it, or rest when you please by giving it some air. The deflatable jacket's disadvantages are that it requires careful handling to avoid punctures and it is useless if you are struck unconscious before reaching your CO_2 charge – as is possible if, for example, you are hit by a speedboat.

Flares, Lights & Reflectors

Each boat should carry its own set of flares. Ideally, this set would include a pack of mini-flares, which may be used to communicate at night, or as a follow-up to a distress rocket. A couple of large parachute flares such as the Schermuly rockets should also be carried. The available range includes a very effective maroon star signal flare and flares with radar reflective payloads.

A flashlight is an even greater necessity – useful for alerting motor boats to your presence, and invaluable for night landings. The best I have found is the plastic two-cell diver's light with the screw-on hood. On especially dangerous coasts, I sometimes carry an additional, more powerful eight-cell light with the switch taped in the "off" position. Another useful light source is the glow stick – a flexible plastic tube containing chemicals and a glass vial. The contents are mixed by bending the tube to break the vial and shaking. The chemical reaction produces a green light which will last eight hours in temperate climates (more in the tropics and less in the

Unwieldy deck loads usually mean that the wrong kayak has
been chosen for the job.

Arctic). Glow sticks provide enough light to make one kayak
visible to another almost a mile away, and they enable you to
read charts and compass without difficulty. They are not
affected by water and produce no heat.

While travelling at night, if you need to sleep but will
be crossing shipping lanes, you can improve your chance of
being seen with a radar reflector. This can be conveniently
displayed aloft on a fishing rod. It is easy to make a multi-

faceted diamond-shaped reflector which folds away flat for storage. Its value is limited on the open ocean since ships will be on the wide range of their radar, but in foggy channels, such as found on the B.C. coast, fishing boats will more readily detect you with such a device.

Checklist of Additional Safety Equipment

– Heliograph or signal mirror. It should be kept in the deck pouch.

– A miniature diver's strobe light to advertise location at night.

– Dyes for marking the sea to increase your visibility to aircraft.

– Smoke canisters, useful for attracting either aircraft or ships by day.

– Shark survival bag. This should be a double-layered plastic sack about 7 feet long and wide enough to take two people. One layer of the sack should be black, and the other bright orange or yellow.

– Bang stick and shells for defense against sharks.

– Solar still or desalinator, especially for tropical voyages.

– Immersion suit, useful mostly in temperate climates and for cold weather.

– Helmet, for dangerous surf.

– Air mattress or sea seat as a life-saving device and for additional flotation during pump and re-entry.

– A square sail, about 6 feet by 5 feet.

– A VHF radio, for kayak-to-kayak communication and emergency contact with aircraft. (The Sarbe 5 is a good though expensive choice. It is a compact quarter-watt VHF transmitter/receiver small enough to fit in a coat pocket, and it is waterproof.)

– Transistor radio for weather forecasts.

Repair Kit

Ideally, each boat should carry its own repair kit containing patching materials for deck and hull – be that fibreglass or fabric – as well as needles, thread, assorted stainless steel bolts, nuts and clamps, aluminum or brass rivets and screws of various sizes. Tools should include long-nosed pliers, a bradawl, screwdriver, small hacksaw, sailmaker's palm, whetstone and spare fittings, and a waterproof zipper suitable for the spray skirt. Several feet of copper wire and some tough monofilament stainless steel wire are also handy, along with enough braided stainless wire to replace both rudder cables. Most useful of all is a roll of refrigeration tape or divers' airhose tape, which is capable of holding the whole show together (and frequently does). The repair kit should be stored, of course, in a waterproof container.

BAGS AND CONTAINERS

Sea canoeing has almost unlimited potential for people who like putting things in bags and sealing them tightly. A good system for waterproofing equipment is crucial, and in cold climates your life may depend on it. The best commercial waterproof bags I have found are the Klepper clothing bags. They have a tough fabric exterior which protects the rubber inner layer. The bags seal by means of a flap and dome-closure. Less expensive, and disproportionately less effective, is a series of garbage bags placed one inside the other with necks folded over and tied. If these are used, they should be protected by a regular canvas bag. Boats with a beam in excess of about 24 inches usually have useful spaces on either side of the seats. These can be used efficiently if specially fitted, zippered bags are built to hold items you may require while paddling. It is much safer than carrying bits and pieces on deck and it is more convenient than carrying them loose inside the boat. Items such as flares, VHF radio, flashlight, diving mask, machete, camera, and of course lunch can all be stored here and, provided that the bags are securely attached to the boat, they will not be lost should you capsize. Be sure the zippers always open forward to aft so that it is easy to open the bags while seated in the boat.

The most efficient food containers I have found are glass mason jars, the kind with the rubber seal, glass lid and wire lever system for closure. (These jars now seem to be made primarily in Europe.) You can see the contents easily, they are watertight, and if you take reasonable care with them they will not break. (We broke only one jar out of sixteen during a six-month trip through the Caribbean.)

The design of food bags will depend on the type of boat you are using. If you are storing your food inside one of the small hatches of a Nordkapp, you may decide to carefully pack the food containers loose and use a bag only for carrying them from boat to campsite. In the larger boats, containers may be carried in a wide-mouthed sack enabling you to rummage about inside the bag for the tin which has migrated to the bottom. It is a good idea to have everything stored in some kind of bag. Apart from securing it during a capsize, it makes carrying easier when your campsite is some distance from the point you were obliged to land.

Several manufacturers now make tapered waterproof bags which fit nicely into the bow and stern of the kayak and which can be blown full of air after loading.

Special attention should be given to a dry bag for your documents. Again, Klepper makes an excellent one. Like their clothes bag, it is tough rubberized canvas with a domed folding flap. Dimensions are 14 inches by 10 inches. The bag has a separate inflation sack built into it so it can also be used to carry a camera and lens without worry of their sinking if dropped overboard. Also on the market are several less expensive plastic and vinyl bags, but these usually have a life span proportional to their economy – not much of a saving when you find your passport or logbook reduced to papier-mâché.

CLOTHING

Paddling generates heat, and even in cold climates, it usually pays to dress lightly so long as the spray skirt is in place and you are wearing waterproofs. I prefer a combination of light woollen underclothing and a light woollen jersey with an anorak and leggings. Rubber boots are convenient but should be removed for long paddles to discourage the formation of mushrooms inside. (Regular dustings with anti-fungal powder will work wonders on these.) If you stop paddling long enough to cool off, have a warm jersey at hand to put on. You will need additional clothing as soon as you get ashore, when the closed kayak is no longer insulating you against the cold.

Even better than the anorak, leggings and rubber boot combination is the Beaufort Mk 10 immersion suit, made of a double layer of proofed Ventile cotton. This garment with built-in boots and rubber neck and wrist seals rather resembles a diver's dry-bag. A heavy duty waterproof zipper across the chest provides access. Condensation is less a problem in the immersion suit than in the anorak combination, and the suit has the great benefit of keeping you dry even when you are *in* the water. The survival advantages of this property can scarcely be overemphasized. The suit is excellent also for sub-zero canoeing, since your body temperature can be regulated by the clothing you wear beneath it. Around camp, these immersion suits are good foul weather clothing with abundant pocket space, and the cuff seals provide dry arms when paddling. My one complaint against the suit is its lack of a hood, though one can be added. (The Mk 10 immersion suits are also prohibitively expensive purchased new but can sometimes be found at reasonable cost in surplus stores.)

Synthetic pile underclothing is quite good for cold weather trips, but where there is a lot of rain or the waves are giving a wet ride, I prefer wool. On a six-month trip in Patagonia, which lasted through mid-winter, I finally abandoned my nylon pile Helly Hansen underclothing in favour of woollen long johns and wool pullover, purchased locally.

One of the joys of warm water kayaking is warm hands. In cold climates you will need pogies or gloves. Pogies are gauntlet mittens designed to cover the closed fists rather than the open hands. They are constructed with a small opening at either side of the fist and a sealable flap across the knuckles so that you can run the paddle shaft in one side and out the other. Pogies will protect your hands while giving you a satisfying barehand grip on the paddle. Many varieties are now available, of either neoprene or nylon, lined or unlined. If need be, woollen mittens with leather palms can be worn inside them.

For cold rain and sleet conditions, ordinary leather workman's gloves are usually adequate, and the wet leather gives a good grip on the paddle shaft. I have experimented with silk inners and rubber outer gloves, neoprene gloves and woollen ones, Millermitts (fingertips cut out) and fancy driving gloves, but simple leather work gloves still seem to be the most practical.

Some kayakers also like to wear spats. These are neoprene tubes which seal the cuffs of your anorak. They make short trips more comfortable but tend to encourage saltwater rashes on longer trips. I have several times started a trip with them only to discard them later and allow the water to flow in and out of my anorak sleeves. Spats are redundant, of course, with immersion suits, and are already sewn onto some specialized paddling jackets.

Kayaking in a wetsuit is not ideal for long trips. Even six hours a day in a wetsuit for days on end is unhealthy and usually unnecessary. For surfing or playing about in boats where there is a high risk of capsize, the suits are well worthwhile, but on a long day's paddle in a seaworthy craft their main use is for emergency survival and when collecting seafood. The farmer-john or overall-style wetsuit, if it is a snug fit, can offer good thermal protection while a self-rescue is carried out, but if you have to survive long periods in the water you will need a neoprene jacket and hood to protect your upper body. Another point: river canoeists can hop behind a hedge whenever nature calls; a sea canoeist has to use a plastic bowl, and getting out of a wetsuit to relieve yourself in a rough sea can be a tricky business.

In the tropics, clothing is mostly for protection from the sun, which for the unprepared can be as deadly as the cold of a northern winter. Cotton is preferable to synthetic, and clothing should be rinsed daily in fresh water if possible to remove accumulated salt. If you are one of those daredevil souls who can look death by skin cancer in the eye, you may get by with a swimsuit during the day; but keep a long-sleeved shirt close at hand for when the sun gets too fierce. A wide-brimmed hat is important no matter how well thatched you might be, and a bandana which can be pulled over the nose and mouth will protect those vulnerable parts. A waterproof anorak and light woollen jersey should be kept handy for rainy or windy night crossings. You may be surprised how cold such a night can be once you have acclimatized to the tropics.

If you expect to encounter difficult surf, you may want one more piece of clothing, namely a protective helmet.

LOADING A KAYAK

Normally it is volume, not weight, that is the limiting factor when loading a touring kayak. Although the manufacturer may claim a boat will carry 250 lbs, the volume of items such as tents, wetsuit, food, clothing and sleeping bag may reduce the effective load to as little as 100 to 150 lbs in a small kayak. A Klepper double can comfortably carry 250 to 300 lbs of regular expedition equipment, and George Dyson's 28-foot baidarkas will take at least half as much again.

How a kayak is loaded is largely a matter of personal preference, but there are some general points to bear in mind. The kayak must ride evenly in the water for normal cruising comfort. A bow-heavy boat will plunge into waves and be awkward to steer, whereas a stern-heavy one will wallow in a following sea. However, if you know you are going to be punching into a head wind all day, it is to your advantage to make the boat light on the bow so that it will rise easily to the waves. Load the objects you will require least frequently in the extremities of the boat, of course, and leave those required at sea or during a lunch stop to be packed last. Everything, both inside and outside, not stashed away in bags should be lashed to the boat.

Spare spray skirts, fittings and emergency food supplies should be pushed as far forward as they will go. Tie a trailing cord around the neck of these bags so they can be withdrawn without having to crawl inside the hull. Heavy objects like canned food, water containers, etc. should be stored along the keel of the boat and some heavy object such as a diver's weight belt kept till last, to correct the final trim.

Carrying a Loaded Kayak

Frequently you will have to move a loaded kayak up or down the beach, which can be hazardous for both boat and self. A loaded double often weighs as much as 400 lbs. Dragging that much weight can damage the hull, and having to push and pull such a heavy load up the beach could strain your back.

If you have four people in your party, the best way to carry a loaded boat is to have two people at each end support its weight on two strops made from nylon webbing slung about 3 feet in from the bow and stern. These strops may be as short as 4 feet, with loops for the hands, or they may be long belts which run over the shoulder and are held in the offside hand. In either case they enable you to carry the boat safely, as the powerful muscles of your legs do the heavy lifting.

One person at each end is much less desirable but often necessary because companions are not handy to help you, or because the surf is too hazardous to leave one boat in it while lugging the other. If possible, remove the heaviest gear from amidships before lifting. This method of carrying is probably responsible for more injuries to muscles and discs than anything else on a kayak journey. It can also put great stress on a boat.

One person, or two people with a strop, can move a heavily loaded kayak up the beach by taking one end of the boat and walking it around 180 degrees, then returning to do the same with the other end. As soon as your boat touches the beach, you can begin this process by lifting the bow and floating the stern up the beach on a wave. To reduce damage to the pivot point, slip a piece of board or an inverted skillet underneath, and let the boat turn on that. Remove or cock the rudder to avoid damage.

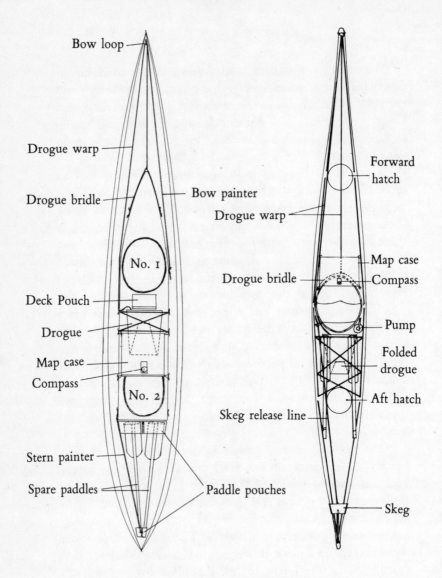

Bow loop

Drogue warp

Drogue bridle

Bow painter

Drogue warp

Forward hatch

No. 1

Deck Pouch

Drogue

Map case

Compass

No. 2

Stern painter

Spare paddles

Paddle pouches

Map case

Compass

Drogue bridle

Pump

Folded drogue

Aft hatch

Skeg release line

Skeg

FIG. 1.7   DECK LOADING OF A CRUISING DOUBLE AND A WEST GREENLAND SINGLE

The Deck Cargo

A well-loaded sea kayak carries the absolute minimum on deck. Nothing which is not firmly tied down should be there unless you can afford to lose it. Convenient as it may be, elastic shock cord is not reliable enough for permanent attachment in rough water and you will eventually lose equipment stored under it.

It is my opinion that the only objects on deck on a long crossing should be spare paddles (in secure holders); a drogue, fully rigged and stored beneath a map case which is made fast at all four corners, and a kangaroo pouch (easily glued to the spray cover) for sunglasses, sweets and the like. Perhaps the only object loosely held by shock cord should be a canvas sack to hold fish caught during the day.

Don't carry your water bottle on deck. It is far too valuable to risk losing, and besides it would heat up in the sun. Flares and flashlight are best stored close inside where they cannot be carried away by a wave or knocked off by another canoe when you are rafted up, and where they will stand a better chance of staying dry.

The after-deck is a tempting place to deposit your treasures, since it is the area least swept by the sea, but it is also the place where you are least likely to notice equipment breaking free. You can even carry rucksacks on the after-deck of some kayaks, at the price of stability, but not during rough or windy conditions and certainly not on open water.

If you are consistently left with equipment which will only go on deck, look to getting a higher volume kayak.

Paul Caffyn and his Nordkapp riding in on a wave on the coast
of New Zealand

2
Technique

PADDLING

The key to long distance cruising is to develop a relatively effortless paddle stroke. This is not possible against strong head winds, but for most other situations, you can ease up on the power as the boat reaches cruising speed. The ideal stroke for steady sea canoeing is a moderately wide, balanced push and pull, with the paddle shaft about 45 degrees to the horizon. The hands are usually held about 24 inches to 30 inches apart. For cruising, unlike racing and slalom canoeing, most of the effort is exerted from the waist up, back braced against the backrest while the knees and feet are lightly braced against the footrest. Over a long haul, the legs and feet are more important for balance than as the roots of power for the stroke. In the West Greenland kayak, the bracing of the legs is more important than in the large cruising doubles, and a footrest is essential to assist with rolling.

To get the paddle stroke right, reach forward an easy distance with the paddle so it enters the water no more than blade depth. Maximum power is exerted during the middle third of the stroke, sweeping out slightly (as demanded by the length of the paddles if they are not to go too deep). This outward sweep will give increased stability. Withdrawal begins as soon as the blade enters the final third of its stroke and is achieved simply by reaching into the next stroke with the opposite paddle blade. Power applied during the last third of the stroke wastes energy by lifting water unnecessarily. The leading arm should punch steadily forward – elbow not quite straight – levering the blade through the water against the pull of the other arm. The fingers of the upper hand should be relaxed and open, the fleshy part of the thumb and palm pushing against the shaft of the paddle. As light a grasp as possible should be maintained with the pulling hand.

On long trips, avoid paddling with unnecessary force. Seek a harmonic rhythm with your partner and the condition of the sea, and try not to succumb to the temptation to race with the boat which is steaming away alongside you. (But if your day is almost over, *then* you can scream "race you to the beach!" and all take off in a wall of spray and thrashing paddles.)

Your travel speed is going to depend on how everyone is feeling as well as on the prevailing conditions. On a long trip at sea, your energy will ebb and flow. Sometimes, for no apparent reason, you will feel like going for it; other times, you will barely be able to push one paddle ahead of the other and wonder why you didn't take up sailing instead. Ride high on the good times by all means, but try not to burn yourself out in mid-crossing. Plodding on with leaden paddles becomes somewhat easier too with the knowledge that the next stage of the cycle is bound to be a good one.

Conserve energy by remembering that you have it. A good trick to try near the end of a long day is to imagine you now have to turn around and paddle all the way back again. (It's great when you don't have to.) Frequently, your energy will evaporate as soon as you make a landfall, and until experience has taught you better, you will be quite convinced that you are incapable of paddling another mile. But if you *had* to paddle back, your energy *would* last. You really have a choice: to let go or to hang on to that energy. The more you hang on to it, the more amazed you will be by the apparently infinite amount at your disposal.

Alone on the sea, your paddle rating will be as variable as the conditions and your mood. In a head wind, it will be long and slow with power applied nearly all the way, sometimes rating under thirty strokes per minute. With a fresh following breeze, you will be doing over sixty, using a chopping, shorter stroke, and your boat will race along.

With wind and waves abeam, you lower your stroke and lean into the wind slightly. The resulting wider sweep stroke on the leeward side will alter the rating slightly. These adjustments will occur automatically as you get used to the conditions. If the waves are big and breaking, a great deal of stability can be acquired by accentuating the regular paddle stroke into the breaking crest, and this may alter your rating as you hang back or jump your stroke to anticipate the whitecap.

Variations in the rating may also occur when running with a good following sea. The waves will alternately push your boat with the crests, then drag heavily at it in the troughs. This speeding up and slowing down can be exhausting. Surfing these waves is good fun, but over distance it is usually best to strive for a steady rhythm.

Chaotic seas, such as those off steep-to lee shores, demand a very rapid rating; you may almost have to sprint through them. Quite likely you'll feel like doing that anyway. You should make your stroke short and quick, providing extra stability in the unpredictable waves. A faster rating leads to faster reactions, readier support strokes and less time spent in unreadable water.

Apart from regular paddle strokes, which offer most of the stability a sea canoeist requires, there are a variety of technical manoeuvres which may be useful.

Sculling Support Stroke

This provides a constant support for a stationary kayak. It stabilizes the boat for operations such as re-entry after a capsize or a dive and is especially useful for doubles. The procedure is to lean the canoe slightly to the side on which you intend to gain support, which should be the weather side when conditions are rough. Leaning downwind increases the chance of capsize. The paddle is stretched abeam the boat and the blade sculled back and forth on the surface, face down, taking enough weight to give stability. This action is most effective if hands are moved about 18 inches back along the shaft towards the airborne blade. This stroke deserves plenty of practice so it won't cut water and send you swimming. It is a useful stroke for emergencies or where an extraordinary amount of stability is required.

Slap Support

As its name suggests, this is a straightforward recovery stroke in which you smack the paddle face (or back) onto the surface to regain lost or threatened balance. It is not used frequently by sea canoeists, but it is a good reflex to develop. The only tricky part is to be sure to slap the face, not the edge, of the paddle onto the water; when you have been varying the feathering of your paddles, your reflex slap just may not be much help to you. A more useful variant of this slap support is to blend the slap into a regular stroke, thus providing recovery power without breaking rhythm. The paddle blade will return to the surface at an angle, so in fact your slap support will lead easily into a sculling support stroke; this gives greater control than a direct upward slice.

The Paddle Brace

Within a breaking wave are upthrusts which you can use for support. A paddle brace involves thrusting the blade into (or onto, if the wave is small enough) the breaking crest so that the blade face rests on the upthrusts while the canoe slides sideways, with you leaning *into* the wave. This is a remarkably stable position. In many boats, it is almost the only way to handle sizeable surf without looping. In its less spectacular form, it can give support at sea when you are caught by a hefty breaking crest. The brace may be either high or low – which is to say, the paddle shaft may be held low across the chest or high above the head.

MANOEUVRING

An efficient rudder is a great asset to a kayak at sea. It saves energy by eliminating the need to break the paddle rhythm for corrective strokes and reduces the chance of your pulling a muscle through uneven effort. But if your boat has no rudder or you need extra steerage, there are other ways to turn.

Sweep Stroke

To adjust your course to starboard, just ease up on the starboard paddle stroke and sweep a little wider with the port stroke while tilting the boat gently onto the port side. To alter course more drastically, skip the starboard stroke altogether and sweep wide to port, or vice versa.

Stern Rudder

This will give you a sharper turn. A stern rudder involves reaching back with the paddle so that the back of the blade bites hard at the passing water, dragging the bow of the canoe around to the paddle side. You lose headway with this stroke.

Reverse Sweep

From the stern rudder position, you can sharpen the turn further by leaning out onto the paddle while at the same time sweeping the blade out and forward across the surface of the water. When the paddle is about 35 degrees off the stern, this stroke becomes a low brace turn or a low telemark, depending on what name you prefer or where you went to school. A high brace turn or high telemark is the same, except that you bring the paddle shaft above your head so that you are virtually hanging from it. The high telemark is a popular stroke with surf canoeists but infrequently used on the open sea.

A reverse sweep, alternating with a forward sweep on the opposite side, will normally turn a single kayak in its own length.

Cross-Paddle Turn

The turning circle of a double may be tightened by a cross-paddle turn. In order to turn sharply to starboard, for instance, the rudder is held hard over while the No. 2 paddler leans back into starboard stern rudder position and then executes a reverse sweep. At the same time, the No. 1 paddler does a forward sweep on the port side. This procedure will normally turn a laden double in its own length.

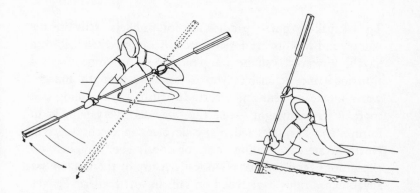

FIG. 2.1 THE SCULLING SUPPORT STROKE, LEFT, AND THE
SCULLING DRAW STROKE

Sculling Draw Stroke

On occasion it is desirable to paddle a boat sideways. The
stroke required resembles the sculling support stroke in many
ways, but you bite deeper with the paddles while hanging off
the shaft in much the same way as you would during a high
brace. Keeping the blade in the water at an angle of about 55
degrees, draw a series of Zs, one on top of the other, and you
will draw the boat beam-on through the water. This manoeuvre is useful to bring one boat alongside another for a lunch
stop, a discussion of charts, or to pass something across. It can
be an indispensable stroke when positioning your boat to assist
a swimmer or capsized fellow kayaker, and is also handy for
docking.

SAILING

To a kayaking purist paddles are for paddlers, sails are for sailors, and motors are for maniacs. An improvised sail on a kayak, however, can be of great benefit in some survival situations since it enables you to conserve strength and cut water intake by reducing effort. In truth, kayak sailing is a sport in its own right – one that was once very popular in Europe and has attracted many devotees in recent years in North America. Sailing can obviously be a relief on expeditions, and indeed, historically many of the longest sea kayak expeditions have relied on sail. In 1911 Frederic Fenger sailed a 17–foot home-built kayak from Grenada to Saba in the West Indies. In 1923 Karl Schott paddled and sailed a Klepper down the Danube to Greece, around the Mediterranean to Suez, and across the Arabian Gulf to India. In 1928 Franz Romer sailed across the Atlantic in a specially built 23–foot single Klepper, and in 1956 Hannes Lindemann repeated Romer's feat in a double.

If you intend sailing your kayak other than running with the wind, some modifications will be necessary. A keel, centreboard or leeboards, as well as substantial ballast, is needed. Several manufacturers sell sailing rigs and leeboards specifically designed for their own sea canoes.

A most remarkable example of an expedition sailing kayak is the *Yakaboo*, designed by Frederic Fenger in 1900 and used on his 1911 cruise of the Lesser Antilles. Fenger, an American of Danish descent, built a cruising kayak which closely resembled those of the late 1960s – and which will, I suspect, have more in common with the kayaks of the 1980s than it has with the slender West Greenland boats in vogue in the 1970s. The *Yakaboo* boasted such features as a self-draining cockpit, watertight bulkheads with hatch covers, a mobile, retractable centreboard and 6 feet of sleeping space. It carried 80 square

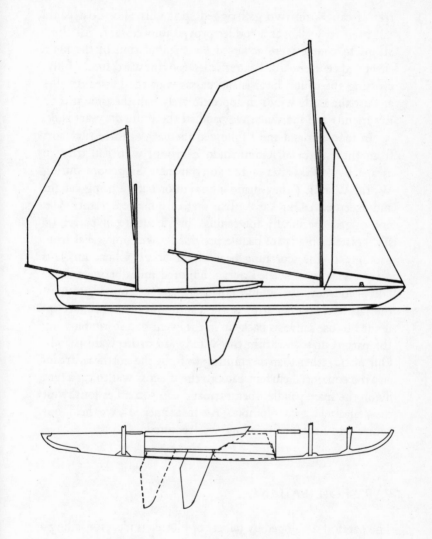

FIG. 2.2 THE YAKABOO: FREDERIC FENGER'S KETCH-RIGGED
SINGLE KAYAK, 17′ LONG WITH A 36″ BEAM

feet of canvas on two gaff-rigged sprit sails. The boat could sail itself so well that a rudder proved unnecessary. All alterations to course were achieved by manipulation of the main sheet and centreboard. Fenger sailed to windward successfully, crossing the rough inter-island passages of the Lesser Antilles against the trade winds in approximately half the time it took my friends and me when we paddled the route 67 years later.

In 1969 a friend and I followed the path of three survivors from the Australian Commando Z-group, who had tried to escape by kayak after a raid on Japanese Singapore during World War II. (They made it to Timor before being caught and executed.) Our kayak, like that of our predecessors, was not rigged specifically for sailing, but a square of parachute silk hoisted on a spare paddle provided a welcome relief from paddling in the scorching heat of the South China and Java seas. Twice we travelled over a hundred miles between landfalls – journeys we would not then have attempted without the sail. On another trip, in the Caribbean in 1977–8, we intended to use sails as a back-up in the event of a storm blowing the party out to sea from the Windward or Leeward islands. Our plan, rather than attempting to fight the northeast trades and the equatorial current back to the islands, was to rig a tent fly on the spare paddle, then turn and run 500 miles southwest to Venezuela or Colombia. As it happened, we held our course and no tent-fly sailing was required.

PARAFOIL SAILING

The parafoil developed by Jalbert of Florida is ideal for sailing a kayak. It eliminates the need for a mast – that source of purchase which can result in a sudden capsize when normal sailing rigs are fitted to kayaks; and it packs away to the size of a shirt.

Above: George Dyson's extremely seaworthy three-man baidarka, whose sail doubles as a tent. Below: A Sandpiper approaches within uneasy range of an Orca pod.

The boat is literally drawn along by the pull on the string. Few kayak sailing rigs are as efficient as paddling into a head wind, so the exclusive use of kites for downwind sailing is no serious disadvantage. In fact, the parafoil can offer assistance to a loaded kayak up to 80° off the wind.

Generally, kites come in two sizes – 7½ square feet and 15 square feet. I also have a 30 square footer (which can almost lift me off the ground in a 25-knot wind), but 15 square feet is adequate to pull even a loaded double when the wind is 10 to 20 knots, and this size is about as big as one can launch from the boat. To launch these smaller kites, I turn the kayak down wind on the rudder, then hold open the tubes on the leading edge. As wind fills them out, the kite lifts and the lines trail through my fingers to the apex, then eventually to the single line.

Although the kite may be flown on 500 feet of line or more it is a lot of work bringing it in again; 75 to 100 feet is usually adequate. Submerged and supported by a buoy on a 6-foot line, the parafoil forms a solid sea anchor.

SURFING AT SEA

In a following sea, when the combinations of wave size, wave shape and boat speed are just right, your kayak will catch the wave and you will find yourself surfing. With practice, you can judge the right moment to throw your weight forward, paddling hard to hitch such a ride. The tell-tale is your bow. Anticipate its burrowing into the wave that has just passed, then haul on the paddles. As the next wave comes up on you, it will lift your bow clear. You can help further at this stage by throwing your weight *back* while increasing your rating as the boat speeds up. Then for a hundred yards or more you can be swept along in front of the wave – at up to three times your normal speed.

The wave passes; your run dies and the boat drags down the back of the wave into the trough. This is not the time to ease up paddling if you want to catch the next wave. Watch your bow, put on full power and throw your weight forward again.

Surfing can heavily tax your strength, but it is a good way to pick up miles at sea and can be grand fun. There will come a time, however, when the fun ceases, the waves suddenly become unmanageable (bad weather seems to sneak up less obtrusively from astern) and you realize, with sudden misgivings, that instead of your playing with the waves, they are playing with you. If you have a boat loaded with fancy equipment (not least your feet) which you are anxious to keep dry, and if the water looks cold and the land is still 15 miles away, you will probably want to alter the rules of the game. When the next big wave builds up on you, stall by back-paddling a stroke or two just at the point where, before, you would have thrown your weight forward. This should not slow you down too much, and it will help prevent that agonizing uncontrolled descent and the distressing high speed broach across the face of the wave, with your weather paddle clawing up the slope towards a wall of green and white about to envelop you.

If you still find your boat being picked up by the waves (a turn of the tide could be steepening their faces) and if you are no longer able to brace comfortably into the breaking crests, you may have to consider a holding action. Turn and face the oncoming crests, paddling into them as they break, and allowing yourself to be blown backward (with occasional help from your paddles). If the wind is strong enough to blow up a sea like that, you will probably still be making in excess of two knots, with your course lying to sternward. Open sea waves can carry very hard-hitting crests. The only ways I know to tackle the really big ones are:

1 paddle right through them;
2 take them side on with your paddle stuck into the turbulence, just as you would come through beach surf; or
3 lie to a drogue.

Once, in very rough water during a night crossing of the Mona Passage, between Puerto Rico and the Dominican Republic, our Klepper was hit by the full force of an ocean breaker while I was busy hand-pumping the bilges. (We had no foot pump.) I sensed the presence of the crest above us and managed to zipper the spray skirt closed just as the wave struck. It came down exactly on our stern, and the force was numbing. My wife, who was the other paddler and who had not seen the wave, at first believed we had been struck by a ship. We were swept totally out of control, though we winged a paddle out on each side as a token gesture. There were four of us, in two doubles, on that trip, and we had been keeping close company. When we shakily regained control after that wave, we were so far away from the other kayak we could barely make out its light.

3
Seamanship & Self-Rescue

Seamanship is the art of living according to the rules of the sea. It is what this book is all about, and it requires, along with knowledge, a healthy respect for the sea and a knack for predicting the unpredictable. It means committing yourself to the problems of the voyage, from initial planning through final execution, with a complete acceptance of responsibility for your actions. Your seamanship is the measure in which you partake of the wisdom of the sea.

DAILY PLANNING

Daily on an expedition you will face the questions of whether and when and where to paddle. These are fundamental questions, always worth re-asking. And as always where the sea is concerned, there are no fixed rules; the variables make every situation totally different. Your choice will depend on the condition of your party, where you are in the world, where you are on the coast, your sense of the weather and of the nature of your intended landfall, how far you will have to paddle to your destination, and how much farther you will have to paddle if you miss it or are unable to land. Timing may be a critical factor, and you may have to choose between a night or daytime trip. A major factor to consider will always be the weather, and more specifically the wind: its direction, strength and likely development. Tides, currents and surf may also require a prominent role in your thinking.

Normally your group will get together for a pre-departure discussion of conditions and the day's schedule. This is the time to talk over all possible problems and decide on a bail-out plan. An escape route should be an integral part of any day's planning. Sometimes one is simply not available and it is particularly important that this fact be realized before you set out, not afterward, when an emergency occurs. Such knowledge will greatly affect your decision to travel or to stay on shore. If your group consists of equally experienced members, you will all be able to decide on the best of several probable alternatives. If, on the other hand, you have one knowledgeable leader this meeting becomes critical in a different way. It allows the group to learn from the leader and understand the reasons behind the decisions. The problems may require less laborious discussion in experienced groups, but a bail-out plan should still always be established and a rendezvous point agreed upon, to be used if the group is accidentally split. Unintentional separations can occur under the calmest water conditions, so before leaving the shelter of a bay, you should agree on your exact destination and a compass course. Even if you can see the land you are paddling to, rain and fog may quickly obscure it. Everyone in the party should know the course and the goal.

It helps to take a day's pause before a big crossing. Spend the time resting, watching weather and currents closely, talking with the local fishermen and eating plenty of good food. Getting the boat and equipment ready in advance is a part of the expedition, as is talking over details of the route with your companions if you have not already worn the subject out. Take some time to compose yourself and quietly go over the chart so that, come the moment to push off, you are totally focussed on the problems to come and have a sound knowledge of what to expect.

TAKING ADVICE

Don't be intimidated by reports of currents that run at terrible speeds. Don't dismiss them either. Just treat all advice on currents with suspicion. Few sailors can accurately report on the speed of currents they have experienced, and seldom do their estimates err on the slow side. This may be because in a motor vessel they usually have far more power available than you do. Likewise, your faithful copy of the government Coast Pilot or Sailing Directions must be regarded only as a general guide to inshore navigation, not as a Bible. For all their survey ships and research stations, navies and coast guards often know precious little about currents.

The best you can do when planning a major crossing is to combine all you have heard and read with what your eyes tell you from the cliff top. Judge each source of information critically against your own experience, then make your decision. Don't let anyone do it for you unless you are listening to a sea canoeist more experienced than you are, or to someone whose credibility you know to be utterly beyond doubt. Yachtsmen's advice must be tempered with your knowledge of kayaks. Commercial fishermen tend to be scornful of sea canoeists, and their advice is often full of gloom. Skippers of ocean-going ships seem to be either all for you or totally against you. Their advice is usually sound, but remember that they don't know the inshore effects of currents, and their ships behave *quite* differently from a kayak in rough seas. Landing sites in particular are a subject on which you cannot unquestioningly accept the word of those who have not studied the coast from a kayak. It may be helpful, though, to cross-examine yachtsmen by asking such questions as: "Can you get ashore in a dinghy?" or "Is it safe to swim in the surf off that beach?" This approach may alter their frame of reference and yield a more useful answer than the general question, "Is there any protection on that shore?"

Remember too, however, that visibility from a kayak is far less than from a yacht or fishing boat, so a sandy cay or rocky reef visible at 15 miles according to yachtsmen may not be visible until 7 miles from your boat.

GROUP TRAVEL

If you are travelling as a group, always stay close enough to maintain communication – unless you have made some other arrangement which everyone clearly understands. During darkness, staying close enough usually means staying within earshot of the other boats and being able to see their lights clearly. Daylight allows travel within hand-signalling distance on fine days, but you should be close enough to respond to likely emergencies during rough conditions.

Although each canoe carries a compass and chart and each person knows the course, it is usually best if one boat leads. This will help to eliminate the tendency crews or solo paddlers have to pull apart, each convinced they are on the right course. I regard this as very important. Diverging compass courses can result from compass differences if some metal or electrical circuit is nearby, but mostly they occur as a result of one helmsman compensating slightly more or less than the others for the effect of each passing wave. It is the sort of thing which can become irritating for everyone concerned, and quite often no one is really to blame – yet the distance can become so great between boats that communication is hampered and someone ends up having to paddle back half a mile to vent off resentment. Another advantage to one boat following the other is that, should the lead boat wander off course, the deviation can quickly be corrected by the other paddlers. It is good for morale if the role of lead boat is changed frequently.

It is the responsibility of the lead boat to see that no one is left too far behind. If you have more than two boats in your group, try to keep one of the strongest paddlers or teams of paddlers at the rear to help in emergencies and to encourage weaker members. Juggle the crews of doubles so that no boat has two weak paddlers. The point of having a team is the additional security the presence of other boats can offer and the pleasure of their company. If you are all going your own ways and not looking after each other, these advantages are cancelled out and you might as well have made your voyage alone.

SELF-RESCUE

Fundamental to safe sea canoeing is a reliable method of self-rescue. It is not good enough to rely on the platitude that there is safety in numbers. Sometimes there is, but it is a fool who bases his capsize recovery on the assistance of companions.

The Eskimo Roll

This is the first line of defense against canning out for those with suitable boats. It is, however, a mistake to rely on the Eskimo roll alone, and one should always be capable of an alternative method. No matter how deft your roll, if you capsize while you have the spray skirt open and your arms inside the boat rummaging for your lunch (a very likely time to capsize), your roll is not going to help you much.

Some kayaks roll easily (some roll too easily!) and others can be rolled only with great difficulty. Some of the surviving traditional Eskimo kayaks are plainly not designed to be rolled, and it seems clear that the Eskimo roll was by no means a universal technique among those who invented and perfected the kayak.

There are many ways to roll and it does not matter very much which one you choose so long as you can do it consistently with your loaded boat. Probably the simplest and most reliable is the Pawlata or extended-paddle roll. It is, I believe, possible to coordinate it for use in doubles, though I have never done so, and with doubles have always relied upon the "marine rescue," discussed a few pages on. For slender singles, the Pawlata is ideal since at sea you have plenty of time to position your paddle carefully.

To learn to roll properly, you are going to need a little help from your friends, or better still from a canoeing instructor. When you are upside down with water up your nose and your world out of focus, it is extremely difficult to be your own best critic on the finer points of the angle and depth of the paddle blade. There are several exercises which can render your first roll a less desperate affair; for a start, you can get used to escaping from an inverted kayak – just in case you should change your mind about rolling some day. Capsize the boat and control your panic. Count to five slowly, then feel

74

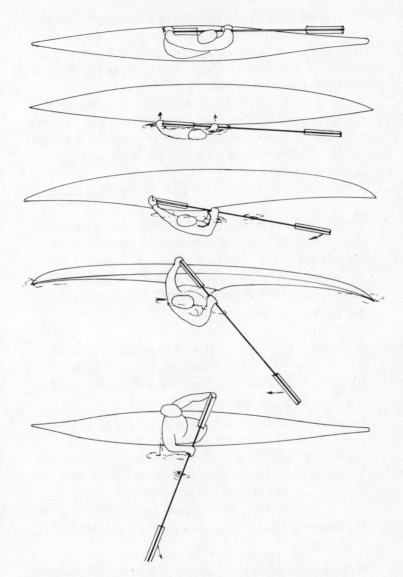

FIG. 3.1 HANS PAWLATA'S VERSION OF THE ESKIMO ROLL

for the spray skirt loops. Count another five seconds, then pull the spray skirt free and do a gentle, unhurried forward roll out of the boat and up to the surface. It is good to know you can come out of your boat without tearing away the deck or leaving your knee-caps behind.

Next, with your friend standing waist deep and holding your hands, capsize and pull yourself upright again. You will find it pays to flick the hips sharply, leaving the head and shoulders to follow. Do this till you can come up easily and without a struggle.

When it's time to make your first attempt at rolling,

1 Lean forward, hold the blade of your paddle in your left hand and, with your right hand, hold the shaft at about the midway point. The paddle is placed along the deck, extended blade towards the bow on the port side, the blade horizontal and facing upward. The right wrist is turned and dropped so the back of your hand faces outward.

2 Capsize the boat and, when you have stabilized upside down, sweep the blade of your paddle towards the surface. At the same time, lean out towards the paddle while pushing the left hand forward and up.

3 Levering the blade against the water at the same angle as that used for a sculling support stroke, sweep the paddle out from the boat. Your head and shoulders will be drawn closer to the surface. As your body begins to break water, pull down hard with the right hand, give a flick with the hips, holding head and shoulders till the last moment, then sculling forward with the paddle for final support.

A list of instructions such as this is a poor, and probably bewildering, substitute for learning from an expert who can see your mistakes and guide you clearly. Most instructors will have their own favoured variations of the roll. What matters is that you find a version you can successfully perform when you have to.

Other Recovery Methods

In this book I deliberately emphasize self-rescue techniques *other* than the Eskimo roll because a back-up technique is mandatory for sea voyages, and because workable alternative techniques are too often neglected. The alternatives taught by most canoeing schools involve the use of one or two other kayaks in a variety of routines with code names such as T, TX, H, HI. These techniques are misleadingly known as *deep water rescues* and basically involve hoisting a flooded kayak across the decks of two others. They have their place as training for novice parties in calm water with empty boats, but they are absurd techniques for the cruising canoeist. They cannot be reliably performed with a loaded boat, and they are hopeless during the sort of conditions likely to cause a capsize. I have myself instructed innocent Outward Bound pupils in these techniques, using the unconvincing line that "with a little more practice you will be able to do it in rough water." That is wrong and dangerous advice, still given by many instructors today.

I repeat that, under rough conditions with loaded kayaks, the classic swimming-pool coaching methods of team rescue simply do not work. Fresh from the factory, a sea kayak may weigh as little as 40 or 50 lbs. Laden with gear and awash from a capsize, it can easily weigh a thousand. A quarter of that weight cannot be handled by two kayakers in calm water, much less a raging sea.

Another method sometimes advocated for sea work is the Eskimo bow rescue. In this procedure, the capsized individual remains seated in the inverted boat, confidently thumping the upturned hull with his fists to attract the attention of his pals. He then sweeps his arms backward and forward in the hope of finding a friendly bow upon which to hoist himself smartly out of the water with a flick of the hips and, doubtless, a loud gasp. Again this can be an interesting exercise. The weakness of the plan (which, incidentally, works fine in a swimming pool) is that it would normally take a good deal more than thirty seconds for a companion boat to be manoeuvred into position to be of assistance. I doubt that anyone who has accidentally capsized at sea will hang around upside down for thirty seconds hoping that this will be the time his mates make it.

Another technique sometimes advocated is the upside-down re-entry for the canoeist who, though capable of rolling, has failed to do so. In this case the individual dives and re-enters the boat upside down (provided the gear has not shifted to prevent this). The spray skirt is then replaced carefully, the paddle manoeuvred into position and the roll executed. All this in a turbulent sea! This again works fine in swimming pools, but it is more of a stunt, a step beyond competence at rolling. It is by no means a method for those who, because of extreme exhaustion or extreme conditions, have just failed to complete the much simpler Eskimo roll.

Pump & Re-entry

There are two versions or stages to this method. The first works well for moderate seas and has been used by the Special Boat Section of the Royal Marines since World War II. Stage two is essentially the same technique adapted for use in heavy seas or very choppy water. Pump and re-entry is the self-rescue method used, in one form or another, by most of the serious and experienced sea kayakers of my aquaintance. In a rollable boat, it is the back-up method, to be used in the event of a failure to roll. In a kayak not suited to rolling, it is the first and last line of defense. I use the Klepper Aerius II as a basis for the detailed examples which follow. A rigid double fitted with cockpit socks is even simpler. Re-entry is naturally trickier in a slender single, and some auxiliary flotation may then be of benefit.

Stage 1

1 As soon as the boat goes over, roll forward out of the cockpit, lifting the spray skirt off by its loop.

2 Check that your partner is clear, that you have both paddles and that the boat is not in danger of being blown away from you.

3 The No. 2 (stern) canoeist gives his paddle to No. 1, who swims to the bow. No. 2 then mantleshelves onto the upturned hull, reaches over, grasps the far gunwale and flips backward into the water, pulling the canoe over with him.

4 No. 2 then re-enters by climbing astride the after-deck while No. 1 steadies the boat by hugging the bow in his arms.

5 No. 2 then steadies the kayak with a sculling support stroke while No. 1 bellycrawls over the bow, finishing the re-entry with a quick pirouette into his cockpit. (This is a vulnerable moment, since balance is precarious. There is also the possibility that gear will have moved during the capsize, making it difficult to re-enter smoothly. There is a case made for No. 1 re-entering first, since the man in the water can offer greater stability than the sculling support stroke. As far as possible, you should check that there is room for your legs before anyone tries to re-enter the boat.)

6 Spray skirts, which you should still be wearing, should be fitted as soon as possible to reduce flooding.

7 The boat is then pumped and bailed dry.

If you are in a lightly loaded kayak, there is a useful alternative procedure for step 3 of this method. Both kayakers dive and come up with their heads inside the boat and their shoulders in the cockpit holes. They inflate their life vests, then grip the coaming and give a synchronized push on one side while holding firm to the other. A light boat flipped in this way will have less water inside and will therefore be faster to pump.

If a second kayak is standing by during re-entry, you will be able to brace your paddle across the two boats, steadying the empty craft and giving you a convenient grip as you hoist yourself out of the water. Lee Moyer of Seattle uses a strop or sling for this purpose, making the re-entry easier yet. The sling is slipped around the hull of the empty kayak and the paddle slipped through the sling athwartships beneath the boat. The second kayak is brought along the far side of the empty one so that the paddle shaft can be braced against the bottom of both hulls. The paddle blade on the near side then becomes a convenient underwater step by which the capsized paddler can hoist himself back into his boat.

The sea, however, has a way of playing havoc with the straightforward antics of Stage 1. You will find that waves constantly sweep over the waterlogged kayak, defying your attempts to pump it dry. The problem is invariably that the boat is too low in the water and one or both of you is going to have to get back into the sea to lighten it. Put on your wetsuits for warmth and your life jackets for extra buoyancy. The procedure is:

Stage 2

1 Re-enter the water, leaving the spray skirts in position on the boat.

2 Unless fresh water is going to be in short supply, the water containers should be emptied then shoved back inside to give extra buoyancy. Air mattresses can be partially inflated inside the boat and heavy objects such as weight-belts and canned food can be ditched or transferred to another boat. All this is so you can pump water out faster than it seeps in, and of course the tighter your boat seals, the fewer problems you will have.

3 No. 2 ties off the No. 1 spray skirt so no water can enter (the bow painter can be used for this), then ties off the No. 2 spray skirt around the hand pump – unless you are using a built-in pump, in which case both spray skirts are tied off.

4 If No. 1 is going to be able to provide an effective deterrent against sharks, he should be wearing mask and fins, not a life jacket. No. 2 can well use the buoyancy of both life jackets so as not to put weight on the boat as he operates the pump. Alternatively you can both pump from the protection of your shark bag.

5 Only when the kayak is floating high should you attempt to re-enter it as described in Stage 1.

A second kayak can help considerably during this operation, but learn to handle it unassisted. Should you fail to pump the kayak dry due to a badly damaged deck or lost spray skirt, you have one more chance if you have a suitable second boat: bring it alongside (waves permitting) and transfer the gear from the middle of the dry kayak to the crippled craft. Then, gaining some stability from the capsized boat, everyone squeezes into the one good boat. This will get you out of the cold water or away from sharks while you wait for conditions to moderate. This four-in-a-boat trick only works with one of the more stable sea kayaks which has an old-style spray cover.

There is no doubt a point during deteriorating conditions when even the Stage 2 heavy-weather rescue will no longer work and attempting to board another boat will mean four of you in the water. Provided that you are relatively warm in your wetsuit, you will probably do best to climb into your combination shark bag/exposure bag, wearing your life jacket. Stay with your boat, holding onto its bow painter unless it is being swept onto rocks or coral, in which case discard your survival bag in favour of your fins and mask, swimming *with* the current along the shore until you are able to get through the breakers. The mask and snorkel will prove useful if you have to take your chances with the surf on rocks, since you will be able to see to avoid most underwater dangers, and the fins will add greatly to the power of your swimming kick.

Buoyancy is the critical factor in any pump and re-entry operation. Anything you can do to increase it will help. Boats with secure watertight bulkheads are better than boats with only flotation bags. Best of all is probably the cockpit sock, since it not only maximizes buoyancy but offers a quick and simple method of draining the cockpit area.

To aid in re-entering the less stable West Greenland style boats, some paddlers use an inflatable mattress or sea seat. The paddle can act as a brace and the boat be entered from the side, much as if you were entering from dockside. A refinement of this has been developed by Matt Broze especially for the Mariner. With some modifications it could be used with most kayaks.

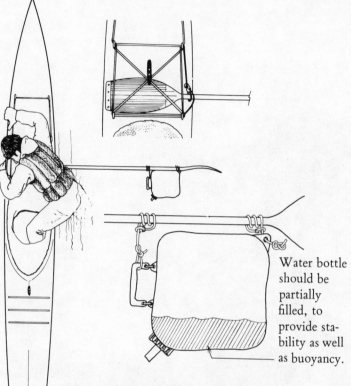

Water bottle should be partially filled, to provide stability as well as buoyancy.

FIG. 3.2 MARINER SELF-RESCUE, DEVELOPED BY MATT BROZE. THIS TECHNIQUE CAN BE ADAPTED FOR USE WITH MOST TOURING KAYAKS. THE SEQUENCE IS AS FOLLOWS:

1 Right the kayak.
2 Slip paddle under the lines aft of the cockpit.
3 Attach water bottle to paddle shaft.
4 If your boat has an adjustable seat, slide it all the way aft.
5 Pull your upper body up on the stern deck.
6 Place one foot in the cockpit, then the other foot, and pivot into the seat.
7 Pump out the boat.

4
Navigation

This chapter is not designed to teach basic navigation. It assumes familiarity with chart and compass, and a degree of competence in basic navigational skills. With that as a basis, the chapter discusses some special difficulties and their solutions using minimal equipment. The kayak, remember, is the smallest, simplest ocean-going craft there is. What I have to say here may well raise the eyebrows of navigators schooled in the methods of a modern navy, but the kayak handles very differently from a motor vessel. The apparent "bush navigator" approach of the following pages is not meant to repudiate precise navigation; rather, it is an acknowledgement of its limits when applied to kayaks at sea.

Most kayak navigation is done by dead reckoning, which in my terms is navigation as an art rather than a science. It involves the use of nautical charts, a watch, dividers, compass, protractor and a great deal of knowledge of weather, tides, currents and wave patterns, all rolled into what eventually becomes an elusive "feel for the sea." You will also need another commodity which can't be found in the chandlery – the knack of turning the answers to old problems into the solutions for new ones. Good dead reckoning means being constantly aware of your approximate position, then using the techniques at your disposal to check and clarify that position. To be unsure of your position on any part of a routine coastal paddle is inexcusable. From your chart, you should be able to anticipate the next problem or the next safe landing. If you find yourself making repeated navigational errors, then brush up fast on your map and compass work.

TOOLS OF THE TRADE

Nautical charts are too large to handle in a kayak. They should be cut carefully into one-foot squares and waterproofed *both* sides with an adhesive clear plastic cover. Take care always to include a section of the corresponding latitudinal degree markings so you can accurately measure distance. Where possible, include a compass rose and make a note of relevant warnings to mariners. For plotting on a plastic-covered chart, use a chinagraph pencil, which can be erased with a cloth or the back of your hand.

British Admiralty charts are usually reliable for deep water readings and sometimes for shallow water ones, but a canoeist cannot always depend on the latter, nor can you always rely on the existence of old landmarks. I have known charts on which not only towns but also whole islands are omitted, lights misplaced and marked channels nonexistent. Perhaps the early cartographers reasoned the waters were too shallow to interest navigators, but small details are of paramount importance to the kayaker. U.S. Defense Mapping Agency charts are usually more accurate, as they are often drawn from aerial photographs. Ordnance survey maps are more reliable for land detail such as roads, buildings and contours, and, where they exist, these maps may be used in conjunction with your chart.

It is not good enough to hold your chart to the deck of the kayak by a piece of shock cord. You cannot afford to lose it of all things. A sturdy canvas folder with a clear plastic window through which the chart can be viewed should be attached firmly to the boat forward of the cockpit. If shock cord loops are fitted to the rear corners, this cover can extend over the spray skirt, where it will offer added protection against breaking waves while holding the chart in the most perfect position to be read as you paddle. The basic Silva or orienteering compass is adequate for a kayak. It can be slipped inside the map case through the velcro-sealed entrance at the rear end of the case. It will eliminate the need for a protractor and is accurate enough for you to paddle to within 5 degrees of your intended course – which is as good as you can reasonably expect from a kayak. Orienteering compasses are inexpensive, and because of their low profile, there is little chance of their being knocked overboard.

Keep a pair of brass dividers in the map case so you can quickly and accurately check distances during the day. It is a good idea to do this frequently against the clock until you have developed a firm sense of speed without constantly having to calculate it.

A diver's watch is ideal for a kayaker and vital for estimation of distances at sea. There are many inexpensive models which are quite adequate.

A radio direction finder (RDF) takes navigation beyond dead reckoning, but it is a useful aid to navigation in certain parts of the world. The coasts of Europe and the U.K. as well as the Bahamas and North America are covered with set frequency transmitters, and a small RDF carried in a kayak can fix your position by tuning in on two of these. I dare say it won't be long before such navigational equipment is available in pocket calculator size.

A sextant and tables is another possible aid for those crossing open ocean or running the risk of being blown out to sea. I have never carried either an RDF or a sextant on any of my trips, though I could have used them on a number of occasions to confirm my dead reckoning. The sextant may also be used for calculating distances by measuring the angles to summits of known altitude, but the bulk of the instrument and its tables makes most canoeists think more than twice before bringing one aboard. Lindemann carried two air force surplus sextants on his Atlantic crossing but finished his crossing by dead reckoning after losing both in capsizes.

TAKING RANGES AND BEARINGS, AND ESTIMATING SPEED AND DISTANCE IN THE WIND

Most sea kayaking is done within sight of land, and the simplest method of locating your position is by ranges or transits. Choose a pair of stationary objects which you can see and which are shown on your chart; then watch for them to *range*, or line up, as you paddle by. A line drawn through the objects on your chart will match the line of sight, the range line through the objects, and your position is necessarily somewhere along that line. If you can gauge the distance to the objects, you can gauge your position. If you combine the range line with a compass bearing on a third object, the intersection on your chart of the range line and the bearing line will give you your position exactly. Even without the compass, you may be able to find two simultaneous ranges, and the intersection of these two lines will again give you a plot of your precise position (see fig. 4.1, example A). Buoys, remember, are likely to move, and should therefore not be used for ranges or bearings if accuracy is required.

Attentive coastal canoeists draw up dozens of mental transit lines as they paddle along. They will notice one object passing another on the shore and not only will they have fixed a mental range line but they also will be able to estimate from

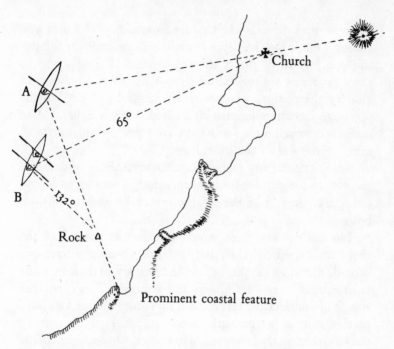

A

65°

B

132°

Rock

Prominent coastal feature

Church

FIG. 4.I DURING COASTAL TRAVEL, KEEP TABS ON YOUR LOCATION BY A SERIES OF FIXES, USING RANGES (A), BEARINGS, (B), OR BOTH.

it how fast the current is running and how much the wind is affecting them. In short, through a vast number of what eventually become automatic ranges, a canoeist can gather a total picture of his progress.

The use of a compass in a kayak introduces some new and exciting ways to make mistakes. Only if you always pack your kayak the same way, and always keep the compass in the same spot, can the compass deviation be reliably known. The fact is, though, you will probably have to move the compass around in order to take bearings. And if you put your flashlight on deck to examine the needle which is to guide you through the foggy dark, your needle will probably be following you instead of the other way around. The solutions to these problems are to load all ferrous metals and radios well clear of the compass and to use a chemical light. With the objective deviation hazard minimized, you will be able to dedicate yourself to a sometimes far more fecund source of error – your use of the instrument.

Some orienteering compasses are conveniently adjusted by the user to compensate for local variation. Take care to correct either the compass or the bearings you take with it, but not both.

Normally a navigator would transfer the bearing to the chart with a parallel rule, and it would be nice to have one aboard, but most kayakers don't and will try to do it by eye – with the aid of two fat fingers and a thumb. This is another source of considerable error! As a substitute for the awkward parallel rule, a perspex grid about 10 inches square can be stored conveniently inside the map holder. Or you may choose to use a combination protractor-plotter instead, correcting all bearings to true and working the protractor against a convenient longitude line.

A useful way to get an approximate idea of your position during a crossing is to get your line of travel by means of a bearing on your point of departure or destination, then estimate your distance along this line by multiplying your time by your known speed of travel. The obvious weakness in this formula is the great variability of "known speed of travel." The following table is a series of estimates based on a standard ten-hour paddle with approximately five minutes' rest each hour and about half an hour for lunch, except in the case of high head winds, where the estimates assume that you must snatch food while paddling. Corrections for current must naturally be made according to conditions.

Wind Speed in knots	Kayak Speed in knots	
20 – 30	1.50 – 0.75	Feathered Paddles
15 – 20	2.25 – 1.50	
10 – 15	2.50 – 2.25	
5 – 10	2.75 – 2.50	
0 – 5	3.00 – 2.75	
0 – 5	3.00 – 3.25	Unfeathered Paddles
5 – 10	3.25 – 3.50	
10 – 20	3.50 – 4.00	Surfing
20 – 30	4.00 – 5.00	

HEAD WIND applies to the upper rows; STERN WIND applies to the lower rows.

A beam wind will usually affect your course, not your rate of travel, unless it is so strong as to interfere with your paddling. Winds forward and aft of the beam naturally have an effect on your speed which varies according to their angle.

OPEN CROSSINGS

The open ocean is normally a friendly environment for a sea kayak. Waves are regular and predictable, winds and currents tend to be constant. Island hopping, which often includes open water, can be trickier, however. You may have a variable current or tidal flow to contend with, disturbed seas on each side of the crossing near land which is exposed to bad weather, and also the big wave exposure of open sea. Part of your planning when island hopping is to gain a clear picture of what the tidal flow will be doing. If local tide tables prove inaccurate, keep a close watch on the ebb and flow yourself. Follow the phases of the moon so you will know when to expect the strongest flows. When you are on the move constantly, you will become as familiar with the phases of the moon and the state of the tide as you normally are with day and night.

Paddling a kayak from one island to another across open sea poses some of the more serious navigational problems you will normally have to face. Let's assume your group is camped on a calm bay on the sheltered side of an island and you plan to paddle 25 miles to a high island due north. You know there is a steady one knot current running from east to west and the wind is forecast at 10 to 15 knots from the east-northeast.

A knowledge of your cruising speed under varying conditions is vital. This information is best obtained not from the foregoing table but from frequent observations and calculation of *your* average speed over a whole day of reasonably constant conditions. A measurement of your speed over an hour or two is meaningless for larger-distance calculations.

Let us say that, in the past, you have calculated your average speed to be 2.5 knots under conditions such as our hypothetical crossing. You know that the 25 nautical miles will take you ten hours. (I would call that eleven just to be on the safe side.) It gets dark at seven o'clock in the evening so you want to be in by five – in case you have to search for a landing or you find yourselves delayed. Counting back eleven hours, your scheduled departure will be for six o'clock in the morning. If your group takes the normal two hours to get away in the mornings, that means getting up at four o'clock.

There is a way of estimating the allowance you will have to make for that one-knot current; take a piece of note paper and rule a line AB 2½ inches long (your Silva compass has a rule on it). This represents your speed, 2.5 knots, at one knot to the inch (and, coincidentally in this case, the distance, 25 miles, at one inch to 10 miles). Then rule a line BC, one inch long, perpendicular to the end of the distance line. This represents the current speed in knots and it is also the distance

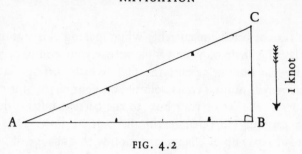

FIG. 4.2

you will be carried off course in ten hours by a one-knot current. Now join the extremities of these two lines to form a right triangle. The acute angle BAC is the allowance you would expect to make to cross this current. The line AC is the distance you can expect to travel, and by measuring this you can calculate your time.

Alas, life is not so simple. Because of your slow cruising speed relative to the current, not to mention the current's variability, you cannot rely on being able to maintain this course. There is usually an allowance to be made for wind, but even neglecting that for the moment, you must take the calculated correction for current as a guide only – one which has to be constantly checked.

Let us assume for example that you depart on schedule and paddle down the sheltered coast to the nearest point of land to your destination. After a brief pause to see that the bilge pumps are sucking water and the spray skirt is correctly secured, you head out into the rough water. Coming from the open sea, the waves are 6 feet and lumpy off the headland due to the current and rebound effect. Paddle steadily on your intended course (in this case due north plus or minus the magnetic variation for the area plus the angle BAC) for a distance of about a half mile. That should take you about ten minutes. Then sight along the shaft of your paddle to your destination (or your departure point, if your destination is beyond the horizon or is obscured). Hold the kayak to your course (as corrected for current) while making this sighting. Then lay the shaft of your paddle across your compass; you should get a reading against the shaft which corresponds to the *uncorrected* compass course plotted on your chart. If it does not, correct the set of your boat to the current until it does. Watch carefully for changes in the current flow. Do you expect it to ease up or change direction with a change of tide? If so, you should know when to expect that change.

Note: It is prudent to err on the weather side of the current and wind during the first part of such a crossing since it is much easier to correct for an overestimation of current than for an underestimation. Once you have decided on a set for the crossing, check it at least once an hour using your paddle shaft. The presence of shoals can greatly affect the speed of the current – pushing a 1.5-knot surface current to as much as 4 knots on occasions. Your chart should show these shoals. Their worst effects can often be avoided by skirting them upstream.

Should rain or haze obscure land, you must combine your total knowledge of all forces affecting your passage, then hold your course accordingly. Have faith in your reasoned decision. The inability to see where you are going can rapidly undermine confidence if you are not prepared for it. Changes of current are difficult to spot unless related to some stationary object such as land or a buoy, but an experienced eye can sometimes detect them from the altered shape of the waves. In the fog your ears will alert you to the proximity of surf, and in rain, visibility is normally sufficient to avoid danger.

Here is an unhypothetical example of navigating by the paddle shaft. There is a 21-mile crossing from Trinidad to Tobago in the West Indies, known as the Galleon Passage. It has a steady current of 2 to 2.5 knots. Our party paddled it at night, going from Toco lighthouse on Trinidad to Scarborough lighthouse on Tobago. Both lighthouses were visi-

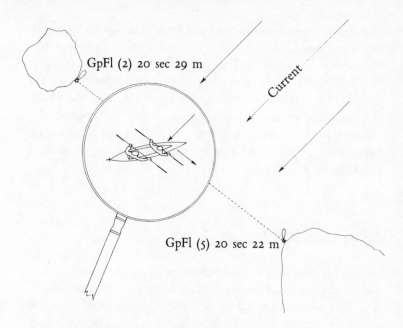

GpFl (2) 20 sec 29 m

Current

GpFl (5) 20 sec 22 m

FIG. 4.3 FERRY-GLIDING ACROSS THE CURRENT

ble the whole way except during brief squalls. Our allowance for the current was frequently as high as 70 degrees from our intended course. Total crossing time: nine hours. Although use of the compass became necessary in squalls, most of the time we simply lined up the two lights along the paddle shafts and varied our set to keep them in line – exactly as a river canoeist would ferry-glide from one bank to another.

A different approach was needed on the next leg of that particular journey, where the distance was far greater: 80 miles of open sea to Grenada, in the Windward Islands. Departure was from a point 65 miles east and 50 miles south of Grenada, paddling due north so as to allow the current to carry us onto the island. This was considerably safer than ferry-gliding as it gave more sea room to correct for unexpected delays – which could not have been made up had we been down-current. Rain obscured our destination until twenty-five hours after leaving Tobago. As soon as a land sighting was made, the course was adjusted to keep upweather of the island, thus assuring seaway for the latter stages of the paddle – a particularly necessary precaution in this case because of a shoal to the southwest, which causes the current to accelerate with nasty overfalls and a poor chance of fighting it back to the island.

MORE ABOUT WIND

Wind can affect the sea canoeist even more than current, but paddle-shaft navigation works for judging its effects as well. The east-northeast wind on our hypothetical crossing a few pages ago could be very difficult for a northbound kayak unless it is fitted with an effective rudder. Craft designed with too much rocker or an imbalanced freeboard windage at bow and stern have the infuriating tendency to turn into such a wind despite every paddling technique you can apply. In this example, however, you would be paddling almost exactly east-northeast by virtue of the allowance you are making for the current, so you need not correct course for the wind at all. You need only take into account that your average speed will be somewhat reduced. The wind, we said, was forecast at 10 to 15 knots, so you could expect it to cut your speed by at least half a knot.

Should the wind swing more to the east, however, you would need to increase the angle of your set by a few degrees to compensate. Just how much allowance you make will depend on a variety of factors, including the weather outlook. Are you trying to gain seaway (getting upweather of your destination)? Has the wind been on the increase? And what is the condition of your party?

If the island to which you are paddling is steep-to and mountainous, be prepared for disturbed gusty winds near the shore, with williwaws, downdrafts and blasts coming from odd directions as a result of the funneling effect down valleys. One such downdraft is the infamous White Squall off the southern end of the island of Dominica, which recently struck a 60–foot yacht so savagely that she was laid hard over. Water flooded through her open hatches and she sank in seconds.

Landforms such as Cabo Froward in the Strait of Magellan so disturb the flow of winds that williwaws, twisters and appalling downdrafts are almost daily occurrences. Indeed, in blustery weather half a dozen or more williwaws may play about the cape at one time.

You cannot expect real progress against a wind in excess of 30 knots. You will barely hold your own against one of 40. But if you paddle at sea long enough, you will sometimes have to contend with even higher winds, especially in squalls, when you may have to settle for a ride backward until the gust eases – at which point you can resume your forward crawl.

One of the worst aspects of really strong head wind is that it prevents you from pausing. Assuming your normal speed is 3 knots, a one-knot headway in a strong wind means you will be blown back at 2 knots if you stop. Seen another way, it means that half an hour's pause in a strong wind demands another full hour of paddling just to regain your previous position. Such conditions can be soul destroying, and these are the situations in which you will be grateful of a small-volume, foot-operated bilge pump, or a large sea-chute, or both.

Normally one would be well advised to avoid making inter-island crossings such as our hypothetical one in winds exceeding 20 knots if they are from the forward quarter. From anywhere astern, however, such a strong breeze may be a great asset – although you will still need to make allowances for drift depending on how close abeam it is blowing.

NAVIGATING IN THE PRESENCE OF COASTAL WINDS

In general terms, coastal paddling may be classified according to whether the wind is onto the land (a lee shore) or off the land (a windward shore).

Unprotected lee shores are normally dangerous. They are usually visited by heavy surf, and may be bristling with rock or coral reefs. The safest thing to have under the surf is, of course, a nice sandy beach. Whenever you are obliged to paddle a lee shore, plan your arrival for certain daylight, and choose as a landing site a sheltered cove or an area protected by an offshore reef. This may not always be possible, and heavy surf may make landing at your intended destination too risky. In that case – if there is no nearby alternative – you have either to continue paddling throughout the night and find a safe landing at dawn, or to search until dark, then anchor offshore and wait until dawn to see what your choices are. Be warned, however, that you should not count on your anchor if the wind is strong, and it is extremely dangerous to attempt to land on an unknown lee shore in the dark.

The sea off a lee shore is usually rougher than open sea, and chaotic rebound waves develop if the coast is at all steep-to. If it is a gently sloping beach, the waves will steepen long before they break. Stay well beyond the line of breakers and keep a weather eye open for the rogue wave which may peak a hundred yards farther out than the rest.

Though it is undeniably dangerous, the lee shore does not hold the same terror for canoeists as it did for the sailors of the old windjammers, whose ships were often swept onto the rocks when they ran out of seaway. Even modern yachts which can beat effectively to windward must take care never to be caught in a gale on a lee shore. You are less at the mercy of the wind in a kayak, but being caught on a lee shore during gale conditions could force you to run unfamiliar surf if there are no good landings within reach, and that is a situation to be avoided if possible. Lee shores without protected harbours should be attempted only when the weather is stable.

Windward shores are more forgiving. The water is calmest here and hazards are more easily seen and avoided. When approaching a small island from upwind, you should land if you can on the windward shore. Even if you *are* able to land on a lee shore because of moderate conditions, you may get stuck there if the wind freshens during your stay. When approaching a strange island in the dark, always do so from the windward shore.

The danger of windward shores is the sometimes strong offshore wind which can blow small boats to sea. This is frequently the cause of fatal miscalculations by the inexperienced who see that the water "looks so calm" close in to land. The farther out you get, the rougher the sea may become and the harder it may be to return. If the wind is really strong you may not be able to return against it from only a few hundred yards offshore. You can paddle a windward shore during high winds only by staying very close to the land. Under such conditions, don't be tempted into taking the short route across a wide bay.

DEALING WITH COASTAL CURRENTS

The sea is seldom without a current along the coast of an island or continent, and you can save a lot of effort if you know what this current is doing. Though annoying, a contrary current on a coastal paddle does not necessarily condemn you to stay in camp. It usually means you should paddle close ashore to gain the benefit of eddies and backflows (though this is not possible on rough lee shores). Even where there *is* a current close inshore, it is frequently slower than farther out to sea. In some cases, shelter can be gained from strong currents by paddling inside the line of kelp or inside a coral reef. Going *with* the current, on the other hand, it is faster to stay well clear of the shore. Entering bays in this case only causes you to get caught up in backflows.

The trick, obviously, is to know when to paddle close ashore, when to paddle out, and, if you are paddling inside the current, to know just how far you have to enter the bays to avoid the head-on current, yet not to lose distance by entering the counterflow too deeply. Your instructions are written on the surface of the sea. Once you realize they are there, they are not difficult to read. Belts of currents can be seen from their effects on the water surface, enabling you to turn tightly into a current flowing your way. Close inshore, snags, kelp, craypot buoys or lines of flotsam may reveal the flow of back eddies which can be of assistance to you. As a cyclist's knowledge of hills becomes more intimate than a motorist's, so your knowledge of currents will become more intimate than other mariners'. Few other craft can navigate in water less than 6 inches deep. And the kayak's slow cruising speed makes an occasional bump on a boulder quite inconsequential if the sea is calm.

NAVIGATING ESTUARIES AND HEADLANDS

Rounding a steep-to headland produces the greatest difficulty for those travelling against the flow of the current. It is off the headland that the current runs strongest and closest to shore. Usually there is no alternative but to sprint around into the relatively still water of the next bay. On a rough lee shore, the current around a prominent headland will produce very turbulent conditions well out to sea. The winds will be stronger and williwaws may occur. In short, headlands are crisis points in coastal canoeing.

Estuaries also produce a variety of surprises for the unwary. Most problems occur in the higher and lower latitudes where tidal variations are greatest and current speeds can get very high if the estuary extends far inland. Where it enters open sea, the tidal outflow from what may basically be a small stream can acquire the proportions of a mighty river. In some places, speeds can exceed 15 knots. Overfalls, upsurges, bores and whirlpools develop, and where the flow meets big ocean swells, rollers form a barrier of destruction. When approaching unknown estuaries, look well ahead for the whitewater, then do what you must to avoid it.

Ferry-gliding is the normal way of crossing a fast tidal flow in an estuary. If you have to make ground against the flow and can't wait for a tide change, stay in as close to shore as you can. If you are going with it, get out in the middle and enjoy the ride. When entering a fast flow from still water, either enter at an angle considerably sharper than that which you will adopt to ferry-glide the stream or lean downstream as you enter the current. This prevents water piling up on the deck and causing a capsize.

NAVIGATING AT NIGHT

Try to avoid paddling by night along unknown coastal waters unless there is a bright full moon or the coast is well marked with lights and lighted buoys. As already mentioned, there are times when night paddling is desirable, but these are usually for open sea crossings or familiar waters. Extra care must go into the planning of night crossings if you are paddling towards an unlit shore. If you can arrange to depart before dark, do so because it will allow you to check your drift against the land before you lose sight of it.

Paddling with your head bowed to the compass all night can be unpleasant. It can also be unsafe, as you will to some extent lose your feel for the sea and increase the risk of seasickness. When the stars are visible, it pays to select one in line with your course and paddle towards it fifteen minutes or so at a time, then select another if the movement of the heavens requires you to do so. Few things can be more enchanting than paddling across open water on a starry night with bursts of phosphorescence glittering on your paddles and streaming off the wet deck. On cloudy nights, you have little choice but to paddle with your eyes to your compass, but when the wind is steady, you may get relief by simply holding a constant angle to the wind and waves. But beware gradual shifts in the wind, made noticeable by its coming to odds with the waves.

The collision rules do not mention kayaks, but they require of a rowboat, "*whether under oars or sail, to have ready at hand a lantern showing a white light, which shall be temporarily exhibited in sufficient time to prevent a collision.*" In addition to a diver's flashlight, I advocate that each boat carry a chemical "glow stick." When we first experimented with these glow sticks, we carried them on the stern of each kayak. In a following sea, however, the light was frequently beneath the water for seconds at a time and on one occasion, a huge fish struck one kayak a blow which the unfortunate paddler described as like being rear-ended at a traffic light. (I have since learned that glow stick lures are popular with deep sea fishermen.) After that, we wore the lights in our hat bands. This increased the effective range of the sticks and provided us with a fine light by which to read the compass.

The great unwritten rule of the sea says that kayaks must get out of other people's way. Lighted or not, your kayak is too small to be seen easily, and you won't appear on most radar unless you are flying a radar reflector. Neither this nor anything else will give comfort in the presence of fast craft such as speedboats, hydrofoils or hovercraft, whose very speed sometimes makes their course almost impossible to predict accurately enough for a canoeist to take effective evasive action. In these cases you will have to rely on your guardian angel and white light, and hope that they are keeping a good watch. This is not to say that big ships cannot be scary and don't travel deceptively fast. They do; but a ship's course is more constant and at night you can tell her direction by the lights – red for port, green for starboard, and the bow light always 15 feet lower than the masthead light. You know all is well so long as you can see only the green or the red light with the two white lights spaced comfortably one before the other. When you see both red and green, and the two white lights one above the other, it is time, or past time, to move quickly.

SNIFFING UP LAND

When paddling over the horizon to a large city or town on a tolerable night you will see the loom of the lights – a glow in the sky – long before you see the lights themselves. The chart will usually indicate the outline of the town, and you can take a useful compass bearing on the glow in the heavens. The loom of a lighthouse too is usually visible well beyond the limit of visibility of the light itself. Your chart will indicate the range at which the *light*, not the loom, can be seen on a clear night. Lights in places such as the Bahamas, Latin America, Southeast Asia and the Middle East cannot be relied upon.

Convection clouds are flat-bottomed fluffy clouds which form above low land masses in the tropics. The morning sun heats the land faster than the sea, and the hot air goes straight up, forming a cloud when the dew point is reached. In the Bahamas, you often see a fluffy replica forming directly above the landmass, most distinct around noon. This airborne model can be so accurate that it shows the individual bays which lie below. By late afternoon, the image will usually have merged into more general cloud, but these too may tell a tale because their bellies reflect the pale turquoise water of The Banks.

Mountain clouds (cumulus rain clouds) often hover around the peaks of high islands, especially in the tropics, on otherwise clear, cloudless days. They too may be seen long before the land itself.

Winds and waves may also indicate the presence of obscured land. A flat island may not be visible from a kayak more than 5 miles distant, but look for waves which seem smaller than you would expect from the existing wind over open sea. If the waves are smaller, their *fetch* (that is, the distance over which the wind raises them) may be shorter, indicating the presence of an island or reef to windward.

An old transistor radio containing an internal dipole antenna can be used to locate the direction of a known radio station. Rotate the radio until it gives the best reception. The station then lies on a line at right angles to the dipole. With luck you will know which way to head along this line.

5
Weather

Generally speaking, canoeists set their own limits on the weather – or, more precisely, the wind – in which they choose to paddle. I don't know the limit of a well-found sea kayak, though I have approached what I believed to be my own limit a number of times. Yet always the limits are nudged forward with the use of better equipment and the application of more skill and determination. Who can say where they lie, or even be sure there are limits at all? I suspect this is the whole hidden quest of the dedicated sea kayaker – the answer to those unanswerable questioners who, without hope of comprehending, ask why you do it.

I say only that if you feel compelled to push your limits in wild weather and rough seas, you must not set out to do it on trips with less experienced people. If you are organizing a group, it pays to view weather defensively. Situations with odds acceptable to one person testing mind and body at sea are often best avoided by a heavily loaded flotilla crossing from one island to another.

It is nice to know, however, that should you be caught in a real blow, all is not lost. You have an excellent chance of survival in a well-found kayak if the paddlers know what they are doing and nobody panics. I once ran before a storm into harbour at Picton, New Zealand, where the weather station was recording winds of 96 knots. We were not blown away and did not lose our paddles or anything else. In fact, the heavily loaded boat handled beautifully. We just clutched the paddles, crouched low and guided her into harbour on the rudder. In the Windward Passage north of Haiti, four of us in two boats were once caught 20 miles from land in a tremendous storm at night. Preceded by a waterspout over a thousand feet high, the wind at one stage did a full 360 degree turn in one hour, and the rain and flying spray were such that it was almost impossible to see the light on the other canoe, although it was so close there was a constant risk of collision. Lindemann and Romer survived days of fierce storm at sea when they crossed the Atlantic, and many an epic has no doubt been silently endured by the hundreds of dedicated sea canoeists the world over. What I am saying is that with care, knowledge, skill, the right boat and plenty of faith in yourself, you can come to terms with the sea in most weather.

If you have doubts about the conditions, usually the best thing is to paddle out and look. Remember, seas are often more chaotic and difficult near headlands and on steep-to lee shores, so you may have to go out a way into the open sea. If you are a party, however, and you as leader have any doubts at all, be prudent. Return and wait for better weather. You can be pretty sure that those with less experience will be having far more doubts than you have, and their very lack of confidence can only increase their vulnerability. (Some novices, on the other hand, are totally fearless even when faced with disastrous conditions, and these people can be equally dangerous to themselves and their companions.)

Part of your expedition planning is a visit to your library to study the weather patterns of the area, in particular the nature of the prevailing winds. Local mariners usually know nothing about the capabilities of kayaks, but they too can be full of valuable tips on the weather. They can tell you the special weather warning signs of the region – mist forming on such and such peak, or the significance of an unusual shift in the wind. Their descriptions of local weather are also likely to be more vivid than the dry jargon you may hear on the official forecast.

Let's face it, though: pride your forecasting ability as you may, your most reliable and commonly available aid in predicting the weather will be your transistor radio. Before entering an area, record the times and frequencies of marine weather forecasts. Get a weather check before any major crossing or lee-shore paddle. In civilized parts of the world, a phone call to the local weather bureau, coast guard or airport will supply you with exactly the information you require, but if you are in the wilderness, you will have to rely on what you see around you to forecast your own weather. (Sometimes even in remote areas your radio will pick up useful satellite information on the location and movement of air masses.)

WIND ORIENTATION

Weather systems entering the area, bringing shifts of wind which would make a crossing hazardous, will likely be your prime concern. Nature provides warnings of these approaching systems. High cirrus clouds (the effect of a jet stream) usually indicate the approach of a low pressure system still a day or two away. Lenticular clouds threatening more immediate high wind, or a suddenly forming high haze, may also reveal a drop in pressure as a new weather system pushes in. Still other signs are a haze ring around the sun or moon or layers of cloud running at different angles to each other.

In the northern hemisphere, depressions contain winds at the lower levels which blow counter-clockwise, while at higher altitudes (3 to 10 miles) winds flow more or less steadily from a westerly direction. Thus by examining the movement of upper and lower cloud levels during unstable

North

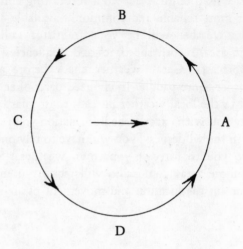

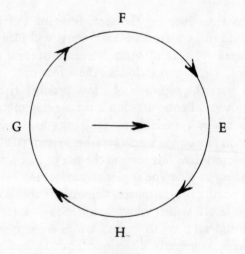

South

FIG. 5.1 WEATHER PREDICTION FROM WIND ORIENTATION. THE DOTTED LINE REPRESENTS THE EQUATOR, THE HORIZONTAL ARROWS REPRESENT THE PREVAILING HIGH-ALTITUDE WESTERLIES, AND THE CIRCLES SHOW THE WIND PATTERNS OF LOW-PRESSURE SYSTEMS NEARER THE EARTH'S SURFACE. AT POINT A, IF YOU STAND WITH YOUR BACK TO THE WIND YOU WILL BE FACING NORTH. THE HIGH CLOUDS WILL BE COMING FROM YOUR LEFT, AND THE ODDS ARE THE WEATHER WILL WORSEN. AT POINT B YOU'LL SEE THE CLOUD LAYERS MOVING IN OPPOSITE DIRECTIONS, A SIGN THAT YOU CAN EXPECT MORE OF THE SAME WEATHER. AT C, IF YOU STAND WITH YOUR BACK TO THE WIND YOU'LL BE FACING SOUTH AND WILL SEE THE HIGH CLOUDS COMING FROM YOUR RIGHT — A SIGN THAT THE WEATHER MAY SOON IMPROVE. AT D, HIGH AND LOW CLOUDS WOULD BE MOVING THE SAME DIRECTION, MEANING MORE OF THE SAME WEATHER.

IN THE SOUTHERN HEMISPHERE, WHERE LOW-PRESSURE SYSTEMS CIRCULATE CLOCKWISE INSTEAD OF COUNTER-CLOCK-WISE, THE SAME PREDICTION RULES APPLY, BUT OBSERVATIONS MUST BE MADE WHILE FACING INTO THE WIND INSTEAD OF AWAY FROM IT. THUS AT POINT E AN OBSERVER FACING NORTH INTO THE WIND WOULD FIND THE HIGH CLOUD COMING FROM HIS LEFT — AN INDICATION OF WORSENING WEATHER. AT F THE HIGH AND LOW CLOUDS WOULD BE MOVING THE SAME DIRECTION, MEANING MORE OF THE SAME WEATHER. AT G, FACING SOUTH INTO THE WIND, AN OBSERVER WOULD FIND THE HIGH CLOUDS COMING IN FROM HIS RIGHT, AUGURING WELL. AT POINT H, THE HIGH AND LOW CLOUDS WOULD SEEM TO BE MOVING IN OPPOSITE DIRECTIONS, AND IT WOULD BE REASONABLE TO EXPECT NO IMMEDIATE CHANGE IN THE WEATHER.

NOT ALL LOW-ALTITUDE WINDS ARE DEPRESSION WINDS, OF COURSE, SO WIND DIRECTION ALONE IS NOT ENOUGH ON WHICH TO BASE YOUR FORECAST. TO AN OBSERVER AT POINT C, A NORTH WIND IS GOOD NEWS, BUT NOT ALL NORTH WINDS IN THE NORTHERN HEMISPHERE PORTEND GOOD WEATHER.

weather, you can locate yourself relative to the depression and can make an enlightened guess at future weather trends.

In the northern hemisphere, turn your *back* to the wind (the direction of the low level clouds) and watch the clouds. If the high altitude clouds are moving in from your left, then you are on the eastern edge of a depression and you can expect a deterioration of conditions. If the high clouds are coming from your right, you are on the western edge of the depression and the weather is about to take a turn for the better. If clouds at the upper and lower levels are travelling parallel, in either opposite or identical directions, you can expect the present weather conditions to persist for a day or two, depending on the size and speed of the depression.

In summary: back to the wind; watch the high cloud; from left is bad; from right is good; forward or backward means no change.

In the southern hemisphere, the situation is the reverse. The high altitude wind or jet stream is still blowing from a predominantly westerly direction, but the depressions in the lower atmosphere contain winds that blow *clockwise*. So the same forecasting rules apply, but you must *face* the wind while you watch the high clouds. If they are moving in from your left, you know things are likely to get worse before they get better.

BAROMETER

After your transistor radio, a barometer is probably the most useful aid to weather prediction you can carry. But the barometer offers no easy answers to weather forecasting. It tells only the present pressure. It's up to you to make an informed guess based on past pressure and apparent trends.

Certainly there is a well-known link between low pressure and bad weather, and the patterns of pressure change can make your prediction better than a wild guess, but even with the knowledge provided by hundreds of barometric pressures over a wide area, the weather services of the world can't claim to have it tabbed – so don't expect too much from your single location readings. Seen in the context of all the other changes going on around you, however, including your wind orientation observations, the behaviour of your barometer should give some meaningful messages.

In the tropics, where the only fluctuation you may get for weeks is the pulse of day and night, a sudden plummeting of pressure is sure indication that you are in for a severe storm. On the coast of British Columbia, Norway, southwestern New Zealand or Patagonian Chile – the lands of the eternal lows – a low barometric pressure may be much less significant, and you will make your decision to paddle or not to paddle according to the wind and wave conditions on the shoreline you hope to travel.

In the temperate zone, where most kayaking is done, there are certain pressure patterns whose predictability makes them worthy of comment. A long steady rise from 980 millibars to above 1020 millibars is a good indication of a stable period of fine weather. Sudden rises seldom lead to long fine periods. A steady fall indicates a more general deterioration. But such rules of thumb should be only one factor in many on which to base your predictions of future weather.

Animals

Animals seem to know when bad weather is approaching. If we humans have lost this sense (though I am by no means sure we have), we can at least keep an eye on other creatures and pay heed to their warnings.

Birds become nervous and more twittery than normal when a big storm is pending. Gulls huddle together on shore, sometimes flying well inland where they squat nervously in the fields or crowd the beaches on little islands.

Sandflies go on an orgy of feeding, and their increased presence is most definitely noticeable.

Mosquitoes tend to be thickest *after* a storm, but if you are in a badly infested area, their pre-storm enthusiasm is also noticeable.

Porpoises have the remarkable trick of leaping clear of the water, then slapping down on the surface with a report like a rifle shot when a storm is imminent. Seeing this, fishermen on the west coast of New Zealand reckon a storm will break within twenty-four hours. I have observed the coincidence there and also in Chile.

Frogs – ah yes, frogs. Such sensitive little creatures. No serious sea canoeist should be without one. Have you ever noticed how excitement and croaking runs high in the frog pond just before the weather is about to break? If you don't have a frog pond near your campsite, why not take a frog along in a mason jar and seek its advice on the weather every morning. It might prove considerably more reliable than some of the other forecasts you will be listening to.

TROPICAL WEATHER

The tropics, regardless of what the tourist brochures may say, are loaded with unsettled, wild weather. Much of this can be anticipated from a study of the weather patterns and an understanding of the basic causes of tropical weather formation; here are a few generalities.

The tropics are an area of prevailing easterlies, usually in the form of the southeast or northeast trades, and you would do well to go with them if possible. In Southeast Asia, the western Pacific and Indian oceans, monsoons have a profound effect. The January monsoon, for example, will provide fresh northeasterly winds until as late as March. A period of southwesterly winds takes over between April and October. Unfortunately, these monsoons don't always follow the text books. I have encountered weeks of near gale-force northeasterlies along the coast of Java during August.

In the Caribbean, December through May is the period of strongest trade wind activity. June through October is the hurricane season, and though the storms are terrible when they strike, they are fortunately rare and the intervening weather usually has long periods of calm.

In Southeast Asia and Indonesia, typhoons strike most frequently between October and December as the July monsoon weakens.

Severe squalls (known as waves) may cause prolonged unsettled weather in the tropics. Visually these resemble the low pressure bad weather of the temperate regions, though there is no barometric variation.

Hurricanes & Typhoons

Let's hope that as a sea canoeist you are not going to be caught out by a hurricane. Unless it forms right over you (in which case you will know about it as soon as the weather satellite), your radio should give you at least a day's warning of its arrival – but don't count on it; keep your eyes peeled for natural signs. If you are in a populated area, you will certainly get the message even if you miss the radio broadcasts. Birds have nothing on people when it comes to flapping! A storm warning of square red flags with black square centres hoisted one above the other at the port entrance (or, at night, a white light between two red lights) is customary, and warnings will usually also be broadcast on a public address system. The sky itself will also be plastered with warnings and the tension will be considerable.

Nature's hurricane warnings:

1 Unusually high swells coming from the direction of the hurricane;

2 Dramatic cirrus displays;

3 A spectacular drop in the barometric pressure;

4 An ominous calm period;

5 Darkening skies which gain a coppery hue;

6 Waterspouts or tornadoes on the right front quadrant six to twelve hours before the arrival of the big winds;

7 Panic among the sea birds;

8 Rapidly increasing wind as the storm approaches;

9 Your weather frog's voice becomes tremulous.

The hurricane is a circular storm (spiraling inward counter-clockwise in the northern hemisphere, clockwise in the southern hemisphere) with winds which may exceed 200 mph. The devastation is staggering. The sea level may rise over 12 feet and waves are very destructive. An expedition of kayakers will have their work cut out surviving on land. Pity help you if you are caught by one at sea, but if you are, you will not be the first. Franz Romer died at sea in a kayak in a large hurricane in 1928. He had just crossed the Atlantic by kayak and had survived two other hurricanes in the course of his crossing.

WEATHER IN THE SUB-POLAR AND THE COOLER TEMPERATE ZONES

Some of the finest canoeing routes are found in the colder latitudes. After all, the kayak is originally a cold weather craft. It seals around your waist, encasing the lower part of your body in still air which acts as an insulator. (Open the spray skirt, however, and the chill factor increases dramatically.)

Western Canada, Alaska, Greenland, Scandinavia and Scotland all provide fine cold weather kayaking. So do Patagonia, the Falkland Islands and the southwest coast of New Zealand. These areas have in common a vulnerability to polar air masses with most of their weather coming off the sea. All were once heavily glaciated, so their coastlines now offer excellent protection and great interest for kayakers in a maze of fjords and rocky islands. They are often remote from the centres of civilization and life is not easy. These areas are subject to constant storms, and a canoeist must be prepared to paddle in all but the very windiest of weather or risk waiting weeks for it to clear. Such latitudes are the breeding grounds of the low pressure systems which invade temperate regions. They can provide snow showers in mid-summer when the sun hovers in the sky for twenty hours a day and the nights don't really get dark at all, whereas in winter you have barely six hours of dim light in which to paddle and the routine of making and breaking camp is done in freezing darkness. One would normally try to avoid paddling during these winter months, but if you are well prepared, there is no reason why you cannot do so.

Patagonian weather, like Alaskan weather, comes mostly from the west, but north and south, of course, are reversed in their significance. Storm winds blast the area from the northwest and bitter polar air masses occasionally sweep in from the south. The southerly wind following the passing of a low pressure system foretells fine weather. Wet westerly winds drop hundreds of inches of rain a year on the tangled mossy forests of the mountain valleys and feed the great Patagonian icecap with an endless supply of snow. The needle of your barometer will mostly oscillate between 980 millibars and 1000 millibars with only the occasional high taking over for a day or two. You mustn't be disconcerted, though, by the bottom dropping out of the glass. Patagonian paddling is so protected that you can almost always find a calm side of a fjord to travel – and as that veteran of Patagonian exploration, the late Eric Shipton, once remarked, "If you wait for good weather in Patagonia, you'll never do anything."

Katabatic Winds & Williwaws

Williwaws result from high winds being deflected by steep land masses. They occur most frequently off headlands which are backed by high mountains or on the fringes of the lee of a high island. These are hardly unique to Patagonia, though the name originates from the region. It is the Yahgan word for the wind squalls of the Magellan Strait. Some of the healthiest specimens may be found frolicking off Cabo Froward. It is a blast of wind, sometimes twisting, sometimes falling out of the sky as a downdraft and rushing across the sea in a wall of spray over 200 feet high. As it travels it collects water from the wave tops and appears as a white cloud. You can hear williwaws coming; at night this is all you have to judge their approach. When they hit, lie low, leaning well into them and holding your paddle so it is not caught by the wind. In an unstable boat, a low profile paddle brace to windward will improve stability. In a stable one, hold your paddle hard against the deck or, if it is feathered, in the water alongside, on the windward side of the boat. This reduces the chances of having it blown out of your hands.

Katabatic winds, or bora, are the result of the drainage of cold air from high ground under the influence of gravity. A vast reservoir of cold air gathers over the icy interior and is tripped by a light offshore wind. It gathers momentum as it avalanches towards the sea. Katabatic winds are common in Greenland, Alaska, Norway, the Antarctic and the Adriatic.

One such wind struck our camp on the shores of the Magellan Strait in 1973. It was a still, moonlit night, and the only warning we had was an eerie howl which brought us out of our tents. The wind almost blew our camp inside out on the first blast. For two hours it slammed into us. Then, as suddenly as it had started, it stopped and there was silence. It is unlikely that vessels at anchor with an eye to protection from the westerly would have survived that devastation from the east.

TEMPERATE WEATHER

The temperate zone, lying as it does between the perennial lows of the subpolar latitudes and the tropical high pressure systems, is the area of greatest unpredictability. It is also, however, the area where you are most likely to get skilled assistance with your weather forecasting, since it is home to the world's most technological civilizations. It is also probably home to most sea canoeists. Here your most important piece of weather forecasting equipment will be your radio or telephone line to the weather office, but you should take care to stay in tune with the signs of nature yourself, since sometimes the edge your guess may have over the weatherman's is that you looked at the sky that morning.

By the way, don't underestimate Mediterranean weather. The summer winds can be fickle and devastating, making long crossings more hazardous than in areas where the wind remains steady. Summer is surely the best time to paddle in the Mediterranean, though I have kayaked there myself only during the winter. It was excellent training for Patagonia – katabatic winds and all.

6
Reading the Sea

Almost everything a canoeist needs to know about the sea is written there in a code of colours, swirls, patterns, shapes and sizes which reflect the weather of the moment and may indicate weather to come. This code can tell you the character of the sea bottom and how far beneath the surface it lies. It can tell you of currents and tides. It may even tell you something of the nearby land. Foremost among the messengers of the sea are the waves – complex pulses of energy which move relentlessly through the oceans. Waves originate chiefly from the action of wind passing over the water, but may also be formed by water flowing over an obstruction, or by earthquakes and landslides (tsunami waves). Their energy is ultimately lost through dissipation as heat – either gradually, due to viscosity, or abruptly, as the wave breaks. With windblown waves, the larger they are, the faster they move.

Remember, though, that what moves is the wave, not the water. The passage of a wave through water does not result in any net movement of the particles of water except where the wave is breaking – and there is little net water movement even then, as the crest tumbles and carries a small surface flow after it. Only the wave energy crosses the seas, while the particles within the wave move in a circle, returning more or less to their original position when the wave has passed.

The waves you will encounter on the open sea will seldom be simple and uniform even when they all appear to be travelling in the same direction. Some waves are obviously

larger than others, and there are moments when the sea almost seems to flatten out. This is the result of waves of different sizes, and therefore different speeds, alternately complementing each other and cancelling each other out. These waves have different origins and their interaction is highly significant for the kayaker trying to get through a line of breakers. By careful observation and counting, a pattern of big and small waves can usually be discerned, enabling you to predict the arrival of the next set of big ones and sneak through before they hit.

Let's have a look at the more common types of wave and how they affect a sea canoeist.

WINDBLOWN WAVES, OCEAN SWELLS AND CHOP

Ocean swells are raised by the wind, but their stormy origin may be hundreds of miles distant. They may exceed 1500 feet in length, from crest to crest, and travel at speeds in excess of 30 knots. As they approach the shallows near land, these great waves steepen and slow. When their height reaches roughly one-seventh of their length, the crests topple and the waves crash ashore as surf.

On the open sea, these waves normally pose little problem to a kayaker. They just slip by, occasionally obscuring the land and other canoeists. They become a problem if you happen to be where they are forming in the midst of a storm; then they can reach their critical height at sea and their crests go plunging down their 50–foot slopes, enveloping all in their path.

Swells also cease to be slumbering giants when they run against a strong current. Under such conditions, the leading face of the swell is undercut, steepens and the crest crashes over as a plunging breaker or ocean roller. Such waves form in the shallows off harbour entrances when there is an outflowing tide, and can occur in the currents of the Gulf Stream and off the east coast of Africa and Japan. This situation is certainly to be avoided since it is extremely difficult to judge the size of the rollers without getting too close. Other places to watch for them include shallow banks fringing deep ocean, and in the estuaries of large volume rivers which flow into open sea. If you cannot avoid these waves, you must handle them as you would surf: head-on if you are going against them, broached-to on a paddle brace or even with a pre-emptive roll (to reduce their destructive impact) if they are abeam.

Windblown waves differ from swells only in that they are smaller and formed locally. They build and die relatively quickly in the open sea, being readily cancelled or altered by a change of wind. They are of shorter wave length than the ocean swells and move correspondingly more slowly.

Their size depends upon the wind speed, fetch (the distance over which the wind raises the waves) and the length of time the wind has been blowing. It also depends on the composition of the water, which in some of the most interesting ocean-kayaking areas is anything but constant. In places the sea may contain hundreds of square miles of fresh surface water, which will cause waves to form more readily and more steeply.

A chop forms where the fetch of the wind is short and equilibrium has not been reached. Such conditions occur in a harbour on a windy day. Chop offers little serious threat to a well-found kayak, though it can be most unpleasant. Steep 3–foot waves are just big enough to throw a bucket of cold water in your face every five seconds when you are paddling into them.

INTERFERENCE WAVES: RIPS, OVERFALLS AND CLAPOTIS

A current setting over a shallow, irregular bottom, or two currents intersecting one another, will often cause a patch of chaotic water called a rip. As the currents responsible for these rips are often tidal currents, the rips are often called tide rips – not to be confused with the so-called riptides, better called rip currents, which are found on beaches. Tide rips and their attendant eddies and whirlpools are notoriously common among the archipelagoes of British Columbia and Alaska, where some but not all of them will be marked on your charts.

Rips are composed largely of standing waves. These are waves which "jog in place," moving up and down while the current flows through them. Standing waves are normally more sharply peaked than travelling waves, and the water in them is for the most part moving up and down and side to side instead of rolling in stationary circles. When these waves break, either from wind or from the force of the current flowing through them, the result is called an *overfall*. These are regularly encountered in Alaska's Alexander Archipelago.

When a wave strikes a steep cliff, either obliquely or directly, it is reflected as if from a mirror. The rebound waves may pass right through the incoming waves, if their crests and troughs do not coincide, but the confused sea which results can make for hair-raising canoeing. When the crests of such contradictory waves *do* coincide, however, their amplitudes combine, creating huge standing waves, again much steeper than travelling waves. This phenomenon is called *clapotis*. (The same word is used on French charts to mark tide rips.)

Off the northern tip of New Zealand, where major wave patterns collide in deep water, clapotis is regularly seen. The pinnacling waves formed here have so much vertical power they can throw a laden kayak clear out of the water. In the Grenadines, between Isle Ronde and Carriacou, is an 8-mile crossing known, for good reason, as Kick'um Jenny. Here the waves often enter both from the Atlantic to the northeast and the Caribbean to the northwest. They strike the steep cliffs at Diamond Head and rebound into a four-way chaos of pinnacling waves for miles out to sea. A current setting side-on at 2 to 3 knots complicates matters still further. The illegible confusion which results can be very rough going in a kayak.

When the current is running hard against normal ocean waves, the wave length shortens and the faces of the waves steepen, causing the crests to tumble. This is another form of overfall, and it too can be very unpleasant for a canoeist. In milder form, however, such conditions usefully betray the movement of the current. Even out of sight of land you can detect a change in the tidal flow from the altered angle and length of the waves. In a kayak during dark night crossings, if the wave patterns are not too confused, you may even feel this change through the seat of your pants.

When the waves become smoother and more rounded than you would expect from a certain wind strength, it is reasonable to expect that they are running *with* the current, though this is more difficult to identify. When the wind blows across the current, the wave length is normal, but the crests are twisted slightly as they break, with a tendency to form toppling pyramids.

A wind blowing against the waves is usually a temporary situation, since waves are normally a product of the wind. When a sudden wind change occurs, however, there can be a period of chaotic seas as the new pattern establishes itself. This is not normally a threat to a kayaker, though it is nice to be prepared for the change when it occurs. Local wind blowing against heavy swells has little effect on the direction or size of the swells. Instead, smaller waves will travel on top of the long swells regardless of their direction. Mostly the chaos caused by wind against waves should be taken as a warning that something unsettling is happening to the weather.

BREAKERS

The way a wave reacts upon reaching land depends on the depth of the offshore waters, the nature of the land and the angle at which the wave strikes it.

Plunging breakers, or dumpers, form where there is a steeply shelving drop-off to open water. There is little shortening of wave length as the wave approaches the shore, and typically there is only one row of breakers which curls and bursts directly onto the foreshore from which the spillage of the previous wave is rapidly receding. From seaward the ferocity of these waves can be gauged by the explosive quality of the break as the air trapped within the plunging crest is compressed and then expands, throwing sand and gravel up with the water. Perhaps the most dangerous plunging breaker is the one that forms on shoals or coral reefs.

Spilling breakers form where the offshore gradient is gentle, and their energy is dissipated gradually. On the north coast of Java, the gradient is so gentle that the waves reach their critical depth miles offshore, and getting out through the surf in the morning can mean a one-hour battle against breakers. Spilling breakers are probably the most manageable for a canoeist, since they lack the explosive quality of dumpers. They also allow you to judge the water depth, since their height declines shoreward in fixed proportion to water depth. (The effect of the tide can be important when planning your landing or departure through these breakers. Where the tidal

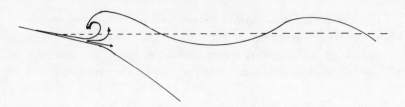

FIG. 6.1 PLUNGING BREAKERS, OR DUMPERS, ABOVE, ARE RECOGNIZABLE FROM SEAWARD BY THEIR VIOLENCE. THEY OCCUR WHERE THE BEACH DROPS OFF STEEPLY. AVOID THEM IF POSSIBLE. IF YOU MUST LAND IN DUMPERS, TRY TO SPRINT IN ON THE BACK OF THEM AND SCRAMBLE OUT OF THE DANGER ZONE.

SPILLING BREAKERS, BELOW, CAN USUALLY BE IDENTIFIED FROM SEAWARD BY THEIR LONG SWEEP TOWARDS SHORE. THE GENTLY SLOPING BOTTOM AGAINST WHICH THEY FORM MAY BE VISIBLE ON YOUR CHART.

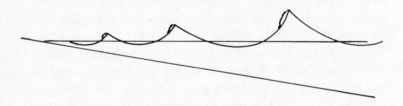

range is great, you may have plunging breakers on the beach at high water and spilling breakers for a quarter of a mile when the tide is out.)

On occasion you will encounter a third type of breaking wave, which occurs when the beach slope just exceeds the steepness of the wave. Then, instead of plunging, the wave surges up the beach, breaking as it climbs.

The distinctions between plunging, spilling and surging breakers are frequently blurred, however, and more than one type of breaker can often be seen on the same beach.

When waves reach land and their energy is not dissipated as breakers, they are variously affected according to the nature

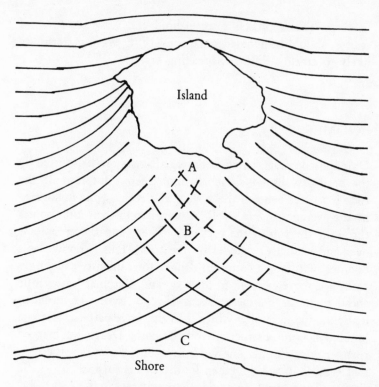

Island

A

B

C

Shore

FIG. 6.2 THE WATER IS CALMEST AT A. B IS A ZONE OF CLAPOTIS AND CHAOTIC SEAS. AT C THE CONVERGING WAVE PATTERNS FOCUS ENERGY ON THE SHORE, CREATING DIFFICULT SURF.

of the land and the angle at which they strike. A small island, for example, causes the waves to change direction and bend around the land mass, spreading their energy as they do so. Standing waves sometimes form behind and somewhat beyond the island, at a distance about equal to the diameter of the island. Here, if the water is shallow and the bottom sandy, a bar will form. When paddling inside such an island it is advisable to choose a course in close to the island. Inside this "wave shadow" is usually the most desirable place to make a landing. The approach from behind the wave shadow, of course, should be avoided since converging wave patterns are likely to create a difficult, breaking sea.

BOOMERS

On exposed coasts, barely submerged rocks can be spotted by the heavy swells which break upon them. But suppose the rock is 10 feet beneath the surface and is not quite uncovered by the average passing swell. A wave larger than usual comes through, the top of the rock is exposed, and the crest folds over and virtually explodes on the rock. This is known as a boomer, and it is a common danger for canoeists paddling a rocky lee shore exposed to open ocean. Watch at least a mile ahead to locate boomers. Eventually you will take an automatic mental note of any breaks in the wave pattern, just as a hiker will note obstructions on the path. Deeply submerged rocks may catch only one wave in twenty – but if you are on that wave you will be taken by disastrous surprise.

Some basic rules to avoid boomers are:

1 Check the chart well in advance and know when currents are likely to push you onto an infested area.

2 If you are paddling through shoal waters, keep a keen eye for and remember the position of all isolated breakers near your course.

3 Avoid patches of kelp which, at higher latitudes, probably conceal rock.

4 If you see rock beneath you, sprint clear.

5 Watch out for waves peaking unusually sharply. They could be "feeling bottom" on a submerged rock.

In the tropics, isolated coral heads can produce boomers. Their position can sometimes be seen from a darkened patch in the sea. Because kayaks frequently travel where no other craft would go you may find yourself in incompletely charted waters. Besides, coral grows, and charts based on fifty-year-old surveys cannot be relied upon to show inshore coral patterns.

WAVES AND WIND SPEED

Waves are the principal tell-tales of the weather at sea, and are used to categorize weather conditions. Waveforms and wind speed as ranked on the Beaufort scale are as follows:

Beaufort Force	Wind	Sea	Wave Pattern and Canoeability
0	0–1 knot	Calm	Monotonous kayaking, risk of hyperthermia in the tropics, old wave patterns only, smooth surface.
1	1–3 knots	Light air	Slight relief from heat unless the movement is from astern; scale-like ripples.
2	4–6 knots	Light breeze	Comfortable kayaking. Small wavelets.
3	7–10 knots	Moderate breeze	Large wavelets; crests start to form and break with clear foam. Good kayaking weather.
4	11–16 knots	Good wind	Small waves becoming longer. Whitecaps. The

			comfortable limit for novice kayaking.
5	17–21 knots	Strong wind	Large waves form; whitecaps are numerous. Weather for experienced kayakers.
6	22–27 knots	Very strong wind	Breaking waves begin to streak; williwaws near headlands. Try to avoid this weather.
7	28–33 knots	Near gale	Moderately high waves with streaks and spray flying from their crests. Not good for normal kayaking.
8	30–40 knots	Gale	High waves, dense streaking and flying spray. This is the practical limit for kayaking (no progress into it).
9	41–47 knots	Strong gale	High waves start to tumble, dense streaking; progress against such wind is impossible.
10	45–55 knots	Storm	Very high waves; long, overhanging crests tumbling. Survival situation running or lying to a drogue.
11	56–63 knots	Violent storm	The sea is white with spray; huge waves. A kayak is running before the wind or lying to a drogue.

12	64–71 knots	Hurricane	The air is filled with foam and spray. Visibility from a kayak greatly reduced.

The preceding table assumes a steady wind on the open sea. In the case of coastal waters and onshore winds, the condition of the waves will be very different, and a canoeist unassisted by technology will have to estimate the wind strength from the appearance of the water surface and the performance of trees, if trees are visible. Gusts are more frequent close to steep land and are especially difficult to estimate.

TIDES AND TIDAL CURRENTS

As there is no shortage of manuals on compass and chart work, so there is no shortage of books on tides and tide prediction. I assume on the reader's part some knowledge of the theory of tides and an ability to use tide and current tables. It is one of the pleasures of kayaking, however, to go where no other boat can go, and this often means going where no tide and current table will lead. At the same time, the kayak, with a cruising speed on the order of 3 knots and a top speed of perhaps 5 or 6, is highly susceptible to the effects of tidal currents. (As a boat which frequently spends the night on a beach, it, like its paddler and his sleeping bag, can also be highly susceptible to the tides themselves.) Current and tide predictions of some sort are indispensable to coastal kayaking, especially in the higher latitudes. This all adds up to the fact that the sea canoeist must develop the primitive sailor's wary and attentive eye for what the water and the moon are doing.

If you are paddling under an opaque Alaskan overcast, your lunar sightings may be few, but if the moon can be seen at all it will foretell much about the state of the tide. Spring tides, of course, come with the new and the full moon. Neap tides occur when the moon is neatly cut in two, at the first and third quarters. The moon's effect increases at perigee (when it is nearest the earth) and decreases at apogee (when it is farthest away). When the perigee coincides with new or full moon, which happens at least twice a year, the tidal range will be particularly large: the high waters will be particularly high, and the adjacent low waters particularly low – perhaps several feet lower than the lows shown on your charts.

High water can be expected a couple of hours after the moon crosses the meridian. At new and full moon, this means somewhat after noon and midnight. At the quarter moon, when the tides are smaller, it means somewhat before. Successive high and low waters are likely to be about equal when the moon is riding the equator. In the Pacific and Indian oceans, the tides tend to be wildly *unequal* when the moon is "in the tropics" – that is, when its orbit runs to the Tropic of Cancer or Capricorn. What this means in terms of the visible declination of the moon naturally depends on where you are when you're looking, but the changes of declination are easily seen, and your tide table should include a lunar calendar which will help you get the hang of it. In thick weather, this calendar alone will give you much of the information you need for seat-of-the-pants tide prediction.

When you have the luxury of using the tables themselves, remember that the predicted heights and times can be drastically altered by high winds. Prolonged or severe barometric drops are generally accompanied by an increase in the tidal range, and a sudden or sustained rise in atmospheric pressure will usually reduce the range. These factors too will cause the tides to depart from the tabulated heights and times.

When you have to negotiate a long passage in which the sea is peaceable only at high or low slack, keep an eye on the tables for a standing tide. This phenomenon occurs when a relatively low high water is followed by a high low water, usually followed again by a low high tide. For hours in such a case the tide may scarcely budge. Standing tides are common at the quarter moon on the Pacific coast of North America.

In other areas, such as the Gulf of California and the South China Sea, the tidal cycle routinely runs at half speed, with only one high and one low water per day, all month long.

Often the item of real concern to a kayaker is not the tide itself but the tidal current. In many narrows and passages along the coast of British Columbia, for example, tidal currents reach 10 to 15 knots. The tide and current tables give current predictions for a few of these channels, but only for a few. The fjords and passages most tempting to the sea canoeist are often precisely those for which no predictions are published. A copy of the relevant U.S. Coast Pilot, British Admiralty Pilot Guide or Canadian Coastal Sailing Directions will often give you a general idea of what to expect. Remember, though, that the coast pilots and pilot guides are not written with kayaks in mind.

Whatever your sources – the coast pilot, published predictions, advice from local fishermen, or casting bones, it is useful to have an advance notion of the set (direction) of flood and ebb currents, their maximum velocity, and the approximate times of slack water. The current may peak anywhere from two to five hours after the turn, but an interval of a little over three hours from slack to peak is most common. The zero current, at the turn, may last only a moment, but for some time before and after the turn, the current will be negligible. How long this slack period will last depends on how fast the current is running when it peaks. At neap tides the current may not be running anywhere near its maximum spring-tide velocity, and the duration of slack water may be much increased. As a general rule, if the current peaks at 2 knots, there will be a period of about sixty minutes at slack water when the current runs at no more than half a knot. If the peak rate is 4 knots, the half-knot slack period is likely to last only about thirty minutes. For a 6–knot current, the half-knot slack may last about twenty minutes, for an 8–knot current fifteen minutes, and for a 10–knot current only ten minutes.

In the archipelagoes of Alaska, British Columbia and Patagonian Chile, the intricacies of tidal currents are such that, by careful planning, a kayaker can paddle around an island on the flood current to a point at which the tidal currents diverge, and, arriving there at high slack, can continue his journey at once, riding the ebb.

With a few significant exceptions, the current will run fastest where the water is deepest. When you are forced to buck the current, therefore, you will usually find it easiest to do so by paddling close ashore. Where shoals or a shallow bar obstruct the main flow, however, the shallow-water current will be faster, not slower, than the deep-water flow. Tide rips and overfalls frequently form in such circumstances, and the current can push you mercilessly through a forest of jagged standing waves. Headlands protruding into the flow will also accelerate it, creating patches of very swift water called tide races. If you are obliged to cross a tidal current, the narrowest part of the channel may therefore be a poor choice. Up-current from a headland or shoal the flow is likely to be less hazardous.

Tide entering a shallow channel may break into a steep-fronted wave called a tidal bore, whose speed is dependent on its height and the water depth ahead of it. Tidal bores may form on expansive mud flats and in tidal rivers. They occur on the coasts of Britain and France, and large ones regularly form in some of the major river entrances of India, Asia and North and South America. A bore 25 feet high advances up the Amazon during spring tides at speeds sometimes exceeding 12 knots. Where bores exist at all, they are usually regular features and will be mentioned in your coast pilot. The large ones can be very dangerous, though smaller ones may provide excellent surfing.

OCEAN CURRENTS

The ocean currents are like great eddies between the continents. They rotate clockwise in the northern hemisphere and counter-clockwise in the southern hemisphere, driven by the spin of the earth and the force of the winds. They have a profound effect not only on tidal flow but also on climate and weather. The relative warmth of the Japan current, for example, is responsible for the mildness of the sea-level temperatures in southeastern Alaska. Ocean currents such as the Gulf Stream off Florida or the Kuroshio off Japan may exceed 4 knots, throwing up dangerous seas when opposed by a strong wind. In the West Indies, the North Equatorial current sieves through the narrow channels of the Windward and Leeward Islands, and into the Caribbean, sometimes running in excess of 3 knots and creating a major navigational problem for craft as limited in speed as a kayak.

In the Mediterranean, a current of quite different origin exists. Rapid evaporation of surface water increases salinity and the denser solution sinks, setting up a deep flow into the Atlantic through the Strait of Gibraltar. The inflow from rivers is not sufficient to compensate for this outflow, and as a result, a steady *surface* flow of Atlantic water runs *eastward* over the top of the deep westward outflow, sweeping the coasts of North Africa and Southern Europe. The entire Mediterranean is said to be flushed through in this manner every seventy-five years.

The author loading a bang stick for protection against sharks in the Caribbean. Beneath the map case is a drogue, folded and ready for use.

7
Hazards

Books like this usually seem to be full of dire warnings of doom. So as not to disappoint you, here is a whole section of doom; but remember, such hazards are only a small part of this game, albeit a crucial one, without which sea kayaking would probably interest a very different sort of person. Sitting at home reading lurid descriptions of freak seas can be intimidating, but it somewhat resembles the panic one feels upon waking suddenly in a car which has braked heavily before a corner: you are confronted by the hazard without the reassurance of the approach. Most sea kayaking is plain paddling, sprinkled with more than its share of euphoric moments.

SURF

Surf is probably the most serious hazard for sea canoeists, who must frequently land and launch on exposed coasts. Surf canoeing can be great fun and is good for building confidence, but it is usually the aim of a cruising kayaker to spend as little time in surf as possible, since his boat is usually loaded with expensive equipment and not really suited for riding breakers. True surf canoeing is a different sport, with different boats, different rules and often different people, but some of its tricks are very useful to the sea kayaker. The most important thing the surfies can teach the sea canoeist is how to judge a wave from seaward – a skill that would otherwise have to be learned through painful and expensive trial and error.

The three main types of surf are discussed in the preceding chapter. Dumpers or plunging breakers are worst and should be avoided where possible, since they can smash your boat to pieces against the sand. If you cannot avoid surf, spilling breakers are your best bet, particularly if there is no explosive quality to the wave as it first breaks. The ideal wave has a crest that collapses well out from the beach, gradually spilling its energy on its way to the land.

Beware of areas where the dissipation of the soup is abruptly completed before the wave reaches land. This smooth area may indicate the presence of a rock or coral shelf with a very shallow layer of water over it. If you come surfing merrily in, you may rip the bottom out of your boat.

Surf seldom breaks evenly on a beach. There will usually be a quieter spot at one or both of the ends of a crescent-shaped bay due to the refraction of waves hitting the beach obliquely. If there is a reef or kelp off the beach, the waves will be broken in the lee of this and you can probably sneak in behind it.

Out Through It

Assessing surf from shore is relatively easy. If you decide the waves are marginal for the experience of your group, you can improve your chances by timing them and counting the sets of big ones. There may be three big then two small followed by five medium – or some similar pattern which will enable you to judge your break for open sea. You may be able to take advantage of a rip current – discussed in more detail a few pages on – to get a fast ride out through the danger zone.

If your group contains any relative novices, these should follow the example of a more experienced paddler, but leave a veteran ashore until last, to help them out if things go wrong in the danger zone. If you only have two boats, send the less experienced boat first so they will have assistance getting off the beach and someone ashore to rescue them if necessary.

If you are travelling in a group, place the first kayak at the edge of the waves with someone from another boat holding the bow into the oncoming soup. The paddlers are made snug and spray skirts secured. When the timing is judged to be right, the person holding the bow pulls the boat past himself, giving it a mighty push into the breakers while at the same time the occupants take to their paddles as hard as they can, gaining sufficient momentum to punch through the wave. Make it a strong steady rhythm till you are well beyond the line of the surf. There you can watch the performance on shore and wait for the party to regroup.

If you are travelling solo or when yours is the last boat, the manoeuvre is a little trickier. Place the canoe at the edge of the surf where it can be reached by the larger waves which sweep up the beach. If you have a double, No. 2 holds the bow while No. 1 (the forward paddler) gets seated and zipped up. No. 2 then quickly slips into the boat and if time allows, makes the spray skirt fast. If the receding wave is already carrying the boat out to sea, the arrangement is necessarily a hasty one since both of you must immediately paddle hard directly into the surf. More often than not you will find yourself sitting in your boat on the wet sand and feeling a little foolish with the sea still 20 feet away. It is just as well. Stay put and arrange your spray skirt snugly. When the next wave reaches you, push off with the paddles or bare hands (not easy with a loaded canoe!). Watch where you put your hands since cuts can be bad news. It is also easy to break a paddle when launching in this manner.

In Through It

Forward is usually the easiest way to come in through surf, but not necessarily the safest when you have a heavily loaded kayak. It involves considerable commitment – perhaps, in view of the difficulty assessing an unfamiliar beach from seaward, a reckless commitment. The great virtue of this method is that it is quick, thus minimizing the time spent in the danger zone. It is a method for heavy surf where you want to get through fast and the beach is clear of obstructions. Let me quote Paul Caffyn (who has paddled the entire formidable west coast of New Zealand) on how he gets a Nordkapp through. "When waves are over 4 feet, I wait offshore and count the sets of big ones going in (usually 3). I wait till a big set is on its way then hammer in behind the last one – casting occasional glances over my shoulder to watch the next set building. This usually gets me past where they are breaking because I'm doing sprint speed of 7 knots or more. When I hear and see the leading breaker of the the following set, I let it get within 20 yards, then I do a right rudder and go into a broach position parallel to the breakers, then lift my paddle into a high brace and lean into the breaker as it hits. It carries Nordkapp in front, sometimes high up the face, but more often on the smooth water immediately in front of the breaker.... On two occasions, I got in through 15–foot surf using this method. By going in at 90° to the beach on steep waves, the bow digs in just as the wave caps, and Nordkapp executes a graceful loop."

When entering sideways through surf, it is essential to lean seaward. Leaning into the land inevitably results in capsize.

Method number two is to go in backward. This technique is useful for unknown or marginal beaches since you are pointed the right way to get out of it fast if you have to. I don't recommend it for crests in excess of 6 feet or for dumping breakers. Once you have chosen an apparently clear path of entry, turn the bow to the oncoming waves. Cock the rudder or skeg clear of the water, then paddle in backward. When the cresting wave approaches, revert to a normal stroke and paddle hard *into* the wave so the boat gathers enough momentum to prevent its being swept backward at great speed. As soon as the wave passes, back-paddle quickly again until the next wave is almost upon you, then repeat. Although this method offers greater control over your entry, it leaves you longer in the danger zone and you can take quite a hammering. As you are going in, you should look over your shoulder frequently to judge distance to obstacles and the beach. In a double, the No. 2 paddler should take this job while No. 1 watches the waves. If you do see a hazard astern, you can usually manoeuvre sideways within the line of surf by ferry-gliding across the flow of the soup.

Method number three: swimming. This is a last-ditch technique, to be used when you must get through exceptionally heavy surf with your equipment dry and intact. It entails getting out of the canoe beyond the surf then swimming it ashore through the breakers. It is only suitable for beaches which are definitely clear of obstructions, and for strong swimmers. Put on either your life jackets and helmets or mask and fins according to preference, then go over the side. Collapse the paddles and stow them inside the boat along with rudder and cables, then seal the cockpit by tying off the entrance to the spray skirt. Even if the boat capsizes, it will take in little water. Swim the boat stern-first towards the beach with one person pushing the bow and the other holding a loop at the end of the bow painter. (Do not put the loop around your wrist in case a wave carries the boat away with you tied to it.) If you keep her going stern first, she should hold into the waves, thus minimizing the drag on the anchor

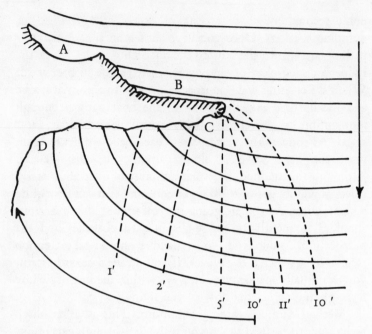

FIG. 7.1 YOU CAN OFTEN PREDICT A SAFE LANDING SITE FROM
YOUR CHART ONCE WAVE DIRECTION IS KNOWN. SITE A HAS
10-FOOT SURF ON THE BEACH AND SHOULD BE AVOIDED. AT SITE
B, STEEP CLIFFS MAKE LANDING IMPOSSIBLE AND WILL CAUSE
CHAOTIC WAVES OFFSHORE. SITE C WOULD OFFER ADEQUATE
PROTECTION FOR MOST PARTIES, WITH WAVES USUALLY 3 FEET OR
LESS. AT SITE D, WAVE STRENGTH WOULD BE DISSIPATED STILL
FURTHER.

man. A good swimmer will find it an advantage to reduce
buoyancy in the life jacket during this operation, so as to duck
below most of the turbulence. The person steadying the boat
should take care never to get "downhill" of the kayak, which
can be lethal in the grip of a big wave.

The way to land in heavy surf on a rocky shore is, don't.
Stay two wavelengths away from the breakline as a precau-

tionary measure while you hunt for a spot where the waves are truly benign or the land less forbiddingly constructed. Derek Hutchinson has suggested a daring technique for surf-landing on rock, which he calls "seal landing." It involves riding up on a breaker, holding at the highest point (assuming you have managed to stay at the front of the wave), then scrambling out quickly and dragging the boat clear of the next wave. This may work for an unloaded boat under surge conditions on pet rocks, but it should not tempt a well-loaded kayaker confronted by real surf and a jagged landscape.

A method I have used for landing on sheer, rocky shores is to search the coast for a protected location. (If you can't find such a place, don't land! You can anchor or paddle on all night if you have to.) Preferably, the shore should be vertical, with a shelf you can reach and no underwater ledges which could catch the canoe and topple it as the wave recedes. Before you can lift the canoe up onto the rock, you have to get rid of most of the weight. One way is for No. 1 to squat in the cockpit while No. 2 edges the kayak close enough to the rocks for him to scramble ashore. (Check to make sure you can pitch your tent there above high tide before unloading all your worldly belongings.) No. 2 then takes out the bags and balances them on the deck or sits them just inside the forward cockpit, then returns with the boat, riding in on a surge to where No. 1 can snatch the bags. The boat is eased clear again as the wave recedes. When the boat is light enough to be handled (it must of course be thoroughly bailed), No. 2 scrambles out on a surge and, with a paddle, holds the boat off the rock while at the same time keeping a hold on the bow painter. The boat can then be brought in on the next suitable surge and man-handled higher as the wave recedes. This method is quite out of the question unless the direct force of the waves is already spent. And don't forget: after a very long crossing, your legs may have trouble supporting your body

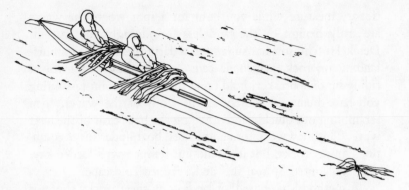

FIG. 7.2   IF THE SHORE IS INHOSPITABLE, A KELP BED MAY BE A
GOOD PLACE TO SPEND THE NIGHT.

weight. They're unlikely to enable you to leap nimbly over
the rocks with your boat.

If you are paddling near beds of bull kelp, you have the
makings for a fine natural anchor should night catch you on an
inhospitable shore. Kelp tends to take the sting out of
breaking waves, and if you can get in behind a dense mat of it,
you will find the waters subdued. Drag the kelp into bunches
and lash it firmly with the bow-line. Sit the boat back on this
and then haul more long fronds over the decks so it is held
fast.

RIP CURRENTS, TIDE RIPS, WIND RIPS
AND WHIRLPOOLS

As surf piles up on the beach, countercurrents form to return
the excess water to the sea. If, as sometimes happens, the
breakers have built a beachfront sandbar, these counterflows
may take the form of rip currents or beach rips – often called
riptides, though since they are not tides and have nothing to

do with tides, this seems a poor name for them. The neck of the rip current is a narrow outflow from the beach, gouging through the sandbar, splitting the breakers and dissipating into the sea beyond them. Its velocity will rarely exceed 2 or 3 knots. Water is supplied to the neck by shallow feeder currents running *across* the beach and into the neck. In a big surf, the feeder currents can be forceful enough to complicate the task of exiting onto unsteady legs from a kayak. The neck of the current, being deeper and stronger, can provide a quick route out to sea from the beach – as unwary swimmers have endlessly discovered.

Tidal currents and tide rips can pose problems of a larger size. As suggested in the previous chapter, swift tidal currents and tide races can so alter the game that, in dealing with them, river experience may be more valuable to you than knowledge of the open sea. Remember to lean your boat *away* from the current as you enter it, and always brace on the down-current side. A bracing stroke to the up-current side will only dump you over. Large tide rips are best dealt with by staying in the middle of the main flow of water if you are going with them or *very* close to shore if you are obliged to fight them. If you have to cross a major tide rip, wait for slack water. For the smaller ones, it is simply a matter of muddling through, watching your balance and, again, leaning your boat away from each new current as you pick your way along. Wind rips, caused by the wind running counter to the current, at least have the advantage that the current is more or less uniform, though the chop can become very steep and unpleasant, readily forming overfalls.

Converging and diverging tidal currents create other hazards as well – eddies, or, in their larger, more frightening form, whirlpools. These you may encounter off points and behind islands even where the surrounding sea appears quite calm, but the small ones are unlikely to do you any harm, and

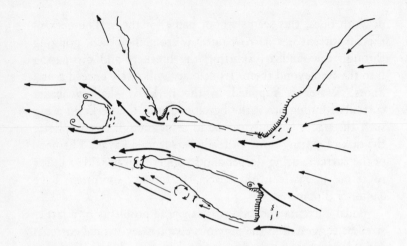

FIG. 7.3 WHERE WATER FLOWS BETWEEN MASSES OF LAND, EDDIES AND BACKFLOWS FORM COMPLEX PATTERNS WHICH MAY ASSIST AS WELL AS HINDER A KAYAKER—ESPECIALLY IF HE IS ABLE TO READ AND ANTICIPATE THEIR FLOW.

of the large ones you are likely to have forewarning. Big whirls will probably appear on your chart and find mention in your coast pilot. They are also likely to be a part of local folklore, so you may hear about them beforehand. It is often worth examining island channels from the cliff top before paddling them.

CORAL

Coral thrives in the warm clean waters between 30° North latitude and 30° South latitude. It forms as long fringe reefs on exposed lee shores and as scattered outcrops on the more sheltered coasts. Each reef is a mass of spiky, jagged calcium formations, often quite close to the surface. It is hard to

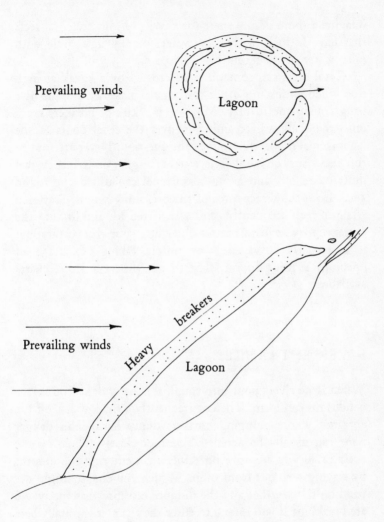

FIG. 7.4 WHAT GOES ONTO A CORAL REEF MUST COME OFF.
THERE WILL BE A RUN-OFF CHANNEL SOMEWHERE — USUALLY ON
THE SIDE OPPOSITE THE PREVAILING WINDS. THE RIP CURRENT IN
THIS CHANNEL MAY BE STRONG, BUT IT IS FAR BETTER TO BUCK
THE CURRENT THAN TO TRY TO SURF OVER THE SAVAGE CORAL.

imagine a more deadly snare for kayaks. Atolls are coral reefs that have formed in shallow water, usually in a circle with calm water in their centre.

Coral reefs can sometimes be crossed by a kayak at high tide when almost no other craft could make it, but this is a dangerous game to play. More often, lines of breakers crash onto the shallows, creaming in over the coral pools to the lagoon, making landing out of the question. Never attempt to run heavy surf on coral. The water that goes on to a coral reef must come off, and a run-off channel can usually be found away from the direct force of the prevailing winds. Scattered offshore reefs frequently offer a sheltered lee and finding the entrance may be just a matter of reading your chart carefully if it is recently surveyed – or simply taking advantage of openings as they appear. Try to get the very latest charts available.

RIVER ENTRANCES

When large rivers pour into rough seas, very dangerous wave conditions can form. There is frequently a shallow bar off the entrance where plunging breakers dump hard. This danger zone can usually be avoided by either closely following the coast or, if you are crossing rather than entering the mouth, by staying well out from shore. Which you choose might depend on the weather and the distance offshore that the waves are breaking. If you intend to enter the river, it is usually best to sneak in via the shallow water on each side of the entrance. Unless the wind is blowing straight upstream, there will be a side of the mouth that receives some shelter from the killing effect the strong current has upon waves. Use this wave shadow if the water is clear of obstructions.

Rivers in flood carry trees and other debris down to the sea. These are often deposited in the muddy shallows near the mouth and may lie just below the surface. It can be most embarrassing if the top of some stake appears through the bottom of your kayak when you are half a mile offshore. Keep a careful lookout.

LIVE HAZARDS

Whales, Dolphins & Porpoises

True whales are not a threat, but since they range up to 80 feet long and weigh as much as a hundred tons, I advocate not provoking them.

The killer whale, or orca (a large dolphin), also seems not to deserve its reputation for being a fierce man-eater. Don Cohen and Alex Lane kayaked recently among a school of between thirty and forty killer whales in Puget Sound. They paddled out to where the whales were cruising up the coast and watched while the vast creatures swam all around them – bulls with 6-foot dorsal fins, cows and young ones. "Sometimes the fins came so close to us the whales had to swerve to avoid touching our boats with the tips," they reported. None of the whales showed any sign of interest in them, friendly or otherwise. They are nonetheless fearsome looking beasts and I have always given them a wide berth. They eat seals, penguins and other creatures nearly my size, and Robert Falcon Scott once watched a pack of them chase his photographer across the ice floes in McMurdo Sound.

Killer whales, humpbacks and others are commonly encountered in British Columbian and Alaskan waters, and in many other good places to be in a kayak. Once in the

Caribbean our kayaks were shadowed for two hours by a shy, apparently amorous humpback. Our first indication of its presence was a piercing, pinging squeak which seemed to be emitting from everywhere at once – a truly nondirectional sound. It was only when the great tail rose in the air several hundred yards ahead that our suspicions were confirmed. It is very exciting to be sharing the sea with such creatures.

Porpoises will often come to investigate a kayak. They are fine company and will not normally harm or upset you, though when playing they may come close enough to clip your hull with their fins. Lindemann, however, reports being almost capsized by large porpoises in mid-Atlantic.

Sharks

It is said that where you have porpoises, you won't get sharks, but don't count on it. Once, off the coast of New Zealand, only a couple of hundred yards from a school of porpoises, I surfed down a wave almost onto the back of a very surprised 12–foot hammerhead.

Sharks do not normally bother a canoeist, but they are a bit like people; there are good ones and bad ones. A kayak is an unfamiliar object to them, and it is rare indeed for one to attack without checking you out pretty carefully first. This checking out process at worst involves a dummy-run bump with the snout, at best a casual glide by. Your instinct will probably be to clout the shark with your paddle and that is no doubt the best thing you could do under most circumstances. Aim for its snout or eye. Don't splash excessively with your paddle, since this may be interpreted as distress and have an effect opposite to the one you intend. The only reliable exception to this comfortable rule is the great white, who, so the story goes, checks you out with a bite. I believe I have had one encounter with one of these. It came at us without any warning in the Tongue of the Ocean (Bahamas), and it was pure chance that my paddle entered the water forcefully just as its snout was speeding towards the middle of our kayak. Maybe the unexpected blow with the paddle put him off his aim enough to miss the first pass, then the commotion we kicked up as I fumbled for the shells for our bang stick checked his confidence and cast doubts on our edibility. Anyway, he turned off at the last moment in making the next few passes.

Wade Doak, a well-known New Zealand diver, found that sharks would not come near a diver wearing a zebra-striped suit. As soon as the striped diver left the water, the sharks were back again. Maybe there is something there for the hulls of sea kayaks. An interesting conclusion of U.S. Navy research into sharks is that the most effective protection for a swimmer is a black survival bag. Experiments with the sharks' reaction to colour revealed that the beasts were liable to attack bright colours such as orange or yellow life jackets. Indeed, one shade of yellow popular with life jacket manufacturers was dubbed by the researchers "yum-yum yellow," because the sharks attacked it so readily.

Discourage sharks by being quietly aggressive with them whenever they come within reach. The greatest risk occurs during a capsize when one is obliged to remain swimming beside the canoe for as much as an hour while a difficult pump and re-entry job is performed. In these circumstances have a diving mask, snorkel and fins close at hand – and carry a bang stick or shark stick (a 4-foot stick with a nail in the end) at all times while paddling tropical waters. It is of course important that the person entrusted with fending off sharks in this manner be a competent free diver, and if this is not the case, you may be better off pumping the boat dry from the protection of your black survival bag.

Sea Snakes

Sea snakes may be encountered in the South China Sea, Java Sea and Indian Ocean, sometimes far out of sight of land. They are usually yellowish brown, seldom more than 4 feet in length, and can be seen lolling lazily on the surface. The main risk for a kayaker is accidentally picking one up on the paddle so it falls aboard, or having one washed onto the boat by a breaking sea. They are non-aggressive creatures, but very venomous. Their bite is fatal in 25 percent of cases and is unusual in that the effects are not felt for as much as two hours after the bite, when paralysis and spasms finally occur. Survivors reportedly recover completely, with no after effects.

Portuguese Men-of-War

The man-of-war is a variety of jellyfish found throughout tropical and temperate zones. It possesses a blue flotation bladder supporting a mass of stinging tentacles which can extend 40 to 60 feet down or, during windy days, may lie along the surface of the sea. The sting is painful and is dangerous to some people, especially if it covers a large area. Normally you will only be caught by the occasional filament swept over the arms and face by breaking waves. The effect does not appear to be more serious than stinging nettle. Some relief can be gained with a topical application of a weak solution of ammonia or antihistamine cream (or simply use urine, which is universally available). Should the stinging be extensive and in a dangerous place, such as the throat, the best treatment is with antihistamine tablets – which should be carried in the deck pouch for just such an emergency. In badly infested waters, it is advisable to wear a long-sleeved shirt, gloves and mask as a preventive measure.

Sea Urchins

There are many varieties of sea urchins around the world's shorelines. All of them should be treated with respect by the lightly shod paddler. Sea urchins affect primarily those obliged to wade ashore across reefs or to launch canoes in shallows. The tropical varieties with long slender spines and remarkable powers of penetration are especially unpleasant. They are found on all sorts of shores except soft mud and are particularly common on coral reefs. Some tropical varieties contain toxin in the shorter spines.

If you are unfortunate enough to get sea urchin spines in your feet or legs, you will doubtless be flooded with earnest advice about dripping candle wax, lemon juice, chicken entrails and goat semen as curatives. Speak politely to all free advisors, then leave the spines alone for a couple of days, disinfect the foot, and dig the blighters out one by one with a needle. Very deep spines will work their way towards the surface over a period of a couple of weeks. A few years ago my wife and I acquired 128 spines in our feet after a capsize on a coral reef. Some spines went right through our feet. None infected, however, and the deepest emerged almost a month after the accident. Note: it is a mistake to attempt to remove the spines with tweezers, since the pressure from the metal jaws will only crush the end of the brittle spine shaft.

Seals, Sea Lions & Walruses

Seals and sea lions can usually be relied upon not to attack unprovoked. If you are on a wilderness expedition that requires hunting sea lions for food, avoid shooting them from the kayak. A wounded sea lion will attack, and one that is shot dead sinks like stone. Walruses are another matter and have a reputation for apparently unprovoked attack.

Jumping & Flying Fish

It is not uncommon to be assailed by dozens of herring or mullet as you paddle through a school of them, usually in shallow water. The shape of the passing kayak panics them into bouncing all over you and the air is heavy with the smell of fish.

Flying fish aboard are a rarer occurrence, though my wife has had the dubious privilege of being slapped in the face by one during a night crossing. As a rule they will fly away from the canoe, but, like garfish, they can fly away from one boat and into the next, or away from a hungry dorado and into you. Flying fish weigh as much as two pounds, so they can give you a nasty surprise. Garfish have substantial swords on their snouts, and there are occasional reports of a venturesome mariner having his cheek pierced by one.

SHIPS AND OTHER MONSTERS

Don't expect to be seen by ships as you sit in your kayak on the sea. You won't even show up on radar unless you have a radar reflector aloft. It is you who must move.

When a ship appears to be coming straight for you, you may find it difficult to decide which side to move to get out of its way. It is worth a few seconds' pause to get it right. Resist the common reaction to scuttle across in front of her; instead, watch the line-up of the bow and the mast closely to see if she is likely to pass in front of you or astern. Then paddle away from the line of her course, taking care to watch the vessel until she is past – just in case she alters course. Don't use flares unless it appears that you truly cannot avoid her course. If you do put a flare up in front of her, she won't alter course, but at least her crew will likely check to see that you are not wrapped around her bows. You don't usually need to worry about the wake of a big ship capsizing a canoe. Tugboats are more of a menace, but seldom so bad as to seriously threaten a competent canoeist. A supertanker at full speed just sends out something like an ocean swell which hardly affects existing wave patterns. Naval vessels under power are another matter: their wakes can be very steep.

Powerboats

These are the bane of the poetic paddler's life. Near marinas, they can be as thick as hornets, and many is the time I have wished my Schermuly flare gun was a bazooka. Some powerboat operators seem to think that if an object is lower than their bows, they will bounce over it if they are going fast enough. Unlike those moving monoliths the merchant ships, small powerboats have the nasty habit of zigzagging and bouncing about so it is almost impossible to anticipate their course if they are heading your way. You never know if they have seen you or not, and there persists to the last instant the fear that the operator will suddenly see one kayak and swerve into another.

Flares are not the answer. Leaving a major port on a weekend may produce close encounters with a score or more powerboats, and you can't go firing off flares every time a boat points your way. Instead, carry a big black garbage bag or an orange survival bag. Keep it handy and when you see the frothing upraised bows headed your way, stuff the bag over your paddle and wave it in the air as high as you can reach. At the same time, turn on your rudder so your boat faces the menace. If it is determined to hit you, at least it will be a glancing blow which will tend to push you aside rather than ride over you. Should a broadside collision be unavoidable, don't hesitate, roll the canoe away from the speedboat and push with your feet against the inside of the canoe so you are projected well below those propellers (not so easy if you are wearing a life jacket). Don't surface till the crashing stops. In some parts of the world (such as Miami) powerboats are the greatest single hazard to sea canoeists. As we approached Miami Beach at the end of a 62-mile crossing of the Gulf Stream, there were speedboats everywhere. Our two kayaks were almost run down by what looked like a brace of bloated 70-MPH slalom canoes. We had unwittingly entered the unmarked lanes of an ocean powerboat race. Boats screamed by within 50 yards of us. One of us fired parachute flares over them, but without effect. We did the only thing we could, which was paddle on through.

Encounters in Fog

When vision is drastically reduced by fog, you have to rely on your compass and ears. When you hear shipping in the fog, paddle gently towards the sound so you have steerage, following the engine noise till it passes. Then resume your course. By keeping your bow towards the source of the sound, you reduce the chances of a dangerous collision. If the source of the sound moves in relation to your compass setting, you are probably safe. If it stays in the same position and is getting louder, you are not. Sounding a whistle is not likely to help you much unless the boat has a very silent engine and an alert watch, though I suppose a fog horn or trumpet might do the trick. Your best defense against shipping in fog is to raise a radar reflector on a fishing pole or some other similar make-shift mast.

One nasty little story on this subject is told by Hilary Collins, who was in a cross-channel party which was almost run down in heavy fog by the Dover to Calais Hovercraft.

ICEBERGS, BERGY BITS AND GROWLERS

Most of the ice encountered on a summer or autumn expedition outside the extreme polar latitudes will be of glacial origin. Icebergs are calved into the sea by hundreds of tidewater glaciers in Greenland, Alaska, Baffin Island, the Svalbard Archipelago and elsewhere in the Arctic, and by several such glaciers in Patagonian Chile. These bergs split and melt into smaller pieces affectionately known as bergy bits (on the order of 500 to 1000 tons), which split and melt into yet smaller pieces called growlers. Since 80 percent to 90 percent of an iceberg is normally below waterline, a bergy bit which looks to be the size of a house may in reality be the size of an apartment block, and a growler which really *is* the size of a house may be awash in medium seas.

For a kayaker, the principal danger inherent in icebergs and bergy bits is that they may calve unexpectedly from a glacier, producing enormous swells, or that anywhere, anytime, they may roll. Icebergs are sometimes beautiful and compelling pieces of sculpture, but anyone who has spent a few days among them must have seen the unpredictable somersaults they perform.

In 1932 the kayak belonging to the talented young British adventurer Gino Watkins was found bobbing in the waves off the coast of Greenland. Watkins himself was not found. It has long been assumed that he boarded an appealing iceberg and caused it to roll.

A domed iceberg has probably rolled already, and you should expect it to roll again at any time. A berg with two distinct horns – a so-called "drydock iceberg" – probably has *not* rolled. It may still be stable, but there is no guarantee. *Tabular* icebergs, which are calved from shelf ice rather than glaciers, are far less likely to roll than the randomly shaped glacial bergs, but tabular bergs are rarely encountered outside the Antarctic Ocean. Floebergs – floes disengaged from the pack ice and drifting along – are also quite stable as a rule, but they are still not to be trusted, because they may calve growlers or floebits (baby floebergs) at any time.

The truly small pieces of ice rubble sometimes found around the faces of tidewater glaciers (or in leads through pack ice) are called *brash*. Remember when paddling among brash ice that, just as with bergs, there is five to ten times as much ice below the surface as there is above it. The pieces are larger than they look, and as you jostle them with your paddle they may jostle you heavily in return.

SEA ICE

In winter and spring, you may well encounter another form of ice: sea ice. During a normal winter, the sea freezes as far south as the coasts of Nova Scotia and Hokkaido, while other waters at far higher latitudes, irrigated by warmer ocean currents, remain ice-free. During very cold winters, ice may form in the North Sea and even in the Adriatic.

The freezing point of seawater depends on its salinity, but as a rule it will be in the vicinity of $-2°C$ ($28°F$). When this temperature is reached and sustained on the ocean's surface, sea ice forms in the following stages:

1 *Frazil.* This consists of minute crystals, giving the sea an oily sheen.
2 *Grease ice.* This is a thin layer of coagulating frazil, more viscous and with a dull or matte surface.
3 *Shuga:* small, woolly, white lumps in the grease ice.
4 *Nilas.* This is an elastic crust several inches thick. It

flexes with the waves but has a definite calming effect on the sea. Thin nilas is dark like the water beneath it, but as it thickens it becomes a light grey and looks something like a mixture of ground glass and paper pulp.

5 *Ice rind:* a thin but brittle crust. As the rind begins to form, it enforces an angular shape on the waves. Under certain conditions, ice rind may form directly from grease ice and shuga, without the intermediary nilas stage.

The first four of these stages are varieties of soft ice. Frazil, grease ice, shuga and dark nilas can all be paddled through – though they will definitely slow you down. A kayaker who continues under these conditions, however, may well find himself beset in ice that is too stiff to paddle through but far too weak to walk on. New sea ice is notoriously weak in comparison with freshwater ice, because it is honeycombed with brine. A thick ice rind may well prevent passage of your kayak *across* the surface and yet do nothing much to prevent your falling *through* the surface. New sea ice as much as a foot thick may be quite inadequate to bear the weight of a man.

As sea ice ages and thickens, the salt gravitates out of it and the ice becomes considerably stronger. Early in this strengthening process the crust is often broken by wave action into relatively small slabs which rub each other round like two-dimensional pebbles. The result is called *pancake ice.* The discs thus formed freeze back together with renewed vigour, and in a few weeks the ice may be sturdy enough to bear enormous loads.

Once sea ice passes the dark nilas stage, it is navigable by kayak only through leads and polynyas. (A polynya is an area of open water in the midst of the icepack.) During the colder

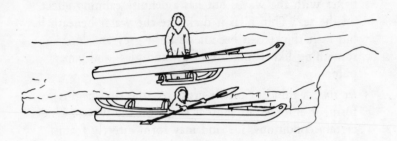

FIG. 7.5 THE KING ISLAND ESKIMO USED SLEDS TO TRANSPORT
THEIR KAYAKS OVER THE SHELF ICE.

months, leads and polynyas may begin to freeze over soon
after they are formed, so that grease ice, shuga and nilas may
be encountered deep in the pack ice in mid-winter or early
spring. A kayaker travelling in such conditions should be
extremely well prepared – not only for sudden immersion in
icy waters but also for camping out on the ice and for an
extended walk across rough ice, pulling the kayak as a sled.
The most insidious danger, however, is that leads can close
just as suddenly as they open. Particularly during the spring or
summer break-up, small leads may grind shut as icefloes or
broken bergs are shifted by current or tide. The American
ecologist and explorer John Muir was nearly crushed to death
in 1890 when he entered a narrow lead in the ice in Glacier
Bay, Alaska, paddling an open dugout canoe.

If you are serious about kayaking in areas subject to sea ice,
you may want to equip your kayak with a sled such as those
used by the King Island Eskimo in the Bering Sea. A light sled
can be carried on the after deck while the boat is in the water,
and strapped beneath the hull for travel across the pack or shelf
ice.

SEA KAYAKING SOLO

To say that a kayaker should not go to sea alone is a bit like saying that someone should not walk in the mountains alone: it is prudent advice, but the reality of sea canoeing is that many of its most dedicated adherents prefer going out alone. The risk is increased, but so are the rewards. It is in the nature of some people to take their own risks and gamble their skill against the sea with their lives as the chips, depending on no one to assist them. It is the ultimate sea canoeing experience, and, because of the greater risk, there is considerable social resistance to it – a resistance not dissimilar to that at first afforded to solo yachtsmen and Alpine climbers. I do not wish through this book to discourage anyone from taking to the sea alone, nor necessarily to encourage them either. Those who truly have the solo canoeing inclination will not be stopped by anything I could say, and do not stand in need of my blessing. I do want to point out the dangers, suggest some precautions and techniques, and make it quite clear that the danger *is* greater. The sea will more readily kill you for your mistakes if you are alone. Above all, a solo canoeist must be capable of self-rescue if he is to survive.

Solo canoeing demands the commitment and serious intent of a high wire walker, bullfighter or solo rock climber. Once you are out there, you are very definitely on your own. I have always prepared for my solo trips by telling nobody I was going – so that nobody expected me back and no one would think to bother the coast guard. Irresponsible in a social sense, perhaps, but in the real sense of the word, totally responsible.

Running before a squall. Note that the paddles are unfeathered to prevent the wind from spinning them, the boat is running between 30° and 45° off the direction of the wind, and the paddlers are ready to brace on the windward side if required.

8

Storm Procedures

It makes sense to think about what could go wrong at sea and what you are going to do if it does.

Storms may be the most common fear of sea canoeists – particularly those attempting difficult passages with many miles of open sea. What do you do if you are caught in a storm? The answers will depend largely on where you are in relation to land, since the best tactic is usually to get ashore. If the land is within your grasp, you may be able to run with the wind to a safe harbour, or, if the wind is blowing athwart your best course, ferry-glide across the storm.

In a severe storm, fighting upwind is out of the question as a means for reaching land. You should avoid wasting energy fighting it unless the storm is expected to be a small one and battling it is seen only as a holding action till the wind drops enough for you to make headway. In such a situation you simply maintain your course as best you can.

Sometimes you will not be able to make land either because the land to leeward is too dangerous or because the only land for a thousand miles lies into the wind. If you have been caught by a major blow and the wind is too strong for you to lift your paddles, or if there is a complicating factor such as a current which will hinder your return to shore, you will have to ride it out. The decision to do so is a critical one and should be acted upon as soon as it becomes clear that this is your best choice, since the object of passively riding out a storm is conservation of strength.

As soon as you realize you cannot escape a storm, check that:

1 All bags and equipment are secure inside the boat;
2 Foot pump and hand pump are both working;
3 The drogue is rigged and ready to go;
4 Food, mask, fins and snorkel are handy;
5 Your emergency locator beacon, if you have one, is at hand.

Then do the following:

6 Tie a loop (figure-of-eight knot) in the bow painter. In a double, tie two – one for each person.

7 Take in all sail and unstep the mast if you were sailing.

8 Put on your wetsuit or immersion suit.

9 Put on your life jacket but don't inflate it.

10 Eat a meal of energy food, drink a little water from each bottle (so they won't sink), relieve yourself, then put a little food in your anorak pocket.

11 Prepare some warps ready for trailing. A 150–foot climbing rope will do nicely, if you happen to be carrying one. Your anchor warp, chain included, will also serve well enough, or a shorter length of line with clothing or almost anything else tied to it to increase the drag.

When you decide to ride the storm out on the open sea, you are again faced with a choice: you can run before the wind or you can lie to a drogue. Your choice is going to depend on what lies to leeward, how strong the wind is, how large the waves are and what your plan is when the storm is over. It will also depend on what sort of boat you are in, and on your previous experience with the different methods.

RUNNING BEFORE A STORM

This is a method suitable for situations where you have a great distance available to leeward or you are running with the wind to a safe harbour. Unfeather your paddles. Turn the boat on the rudder and steer a course about 45° off the direction of wind and waves. Vary this angle according to your relative comfort or lack of it with the size of the waves. Try to avoid surfing directly down the wave face. You may decide to trail your prepared warps at this stage. Have your paddles ready to brace into any heavily breaking crests. Normally, the paddles should be held across the coaming, with the blades tilted forward so the wind pressure holds them down, but you may prefer to trail them on the windward side, thus reducing windage and placing you in a position for ready support.

As the wind increases, lean forward or snuggle lower in the boat to reduce windage and lower your centre of gravity. If your boat does not roll efficiently, hold the bow-painter loop in your hand so that if you go over you will still have a hold on the boat. It might otherwise be blown beyond your reach by the time you surface. Normally it is not advisable to tie paddles to a boat since there is a risk of entanglement, but in this case you have to balance that concern against the risk of losing a paddle as you struggle to stay with the upturned boat. In a single, you may want to tie the paddle to the bow painter so that, in the event of a capsize, you have only to hold onto your paddle in order to hold onto the boat.

LYING TO A DROGUE

Lying to a drogue is useful in the open sea, or when you plan to return to windward after the storm, or where it is

FIG. 8.1   A DROGUE OFF THE BOW WILL HOLD THE BOW INTO
THE WIND AND REDUCE DRIFT. IF A SEA-CHUTE IS USED, A FLOAT
SHOULD BE ATTACHED TO PREVENT THE CHUTE FROM SINKING

important to reduce drift because of a dangerous lee shore. There is considerable disagreement amongst bar-stool sailors at the yacht club concerning the use of drogues during a storm. It is generally conceded that they are fine for reducing drift, under average conditions, but their use in a severe storm is hotly debated. So be it with kayaks.

In theory, a well-set drogue off the bow of a kayak will hold her head into the weather. This is indeed the case with a sea-chute, but with a standard sea-anchor of traditional dimensions the boat yaws badly in its backward drift unless fitted with a counterforce off the stern. Another kayak is such a force, as we discovered while rigged in series for sleeping one night during a fresh wind. The boat at the end of the series yawed wildly as usual, while the kayak to whose stern she was attached held steady in the waves.

It is important to tilt the rudder or skeg clear of the water when you are lying to a standard drogue, since you will still be going backward quite fast. Hold the paddle so it won't be blown out of your hands, or lash it firmly along the deck.

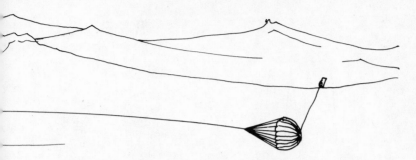

TOO LOW. A DROGUE WHICH ALLOWS SIGNIFICANT DRIFT WILL
CAUSE THE BOAT TO YAW UNLESS A COUNTERFORCE — SUCH AS A
SECOND KAYAK — IS TETHERED ASTERN.

During a gale, far more spray hits a canoeist than would
hit a yachtsman. The yachtsman, no matter how small his
vessel, sits higher out of the water. With the drogue off the
bow you will be facing the wind and you run the risk of being
blinded by spray. A diving mask will protect your eyes, and
you can draw breath inside your parka lip. This arrangement
can also be of assistance when you near the limit of paddlable
conditions or where an imminent lee shore demands that you
claw your way along the coast by ferry-gliding against the
wind to a place where you can land. To increase your stability
and reduce wind resistance, snuggle low into your boat so
only your shoulders, arms and head are above the coaming.
Keep the bilges pumped dry. Lindemann, on his Atlantic
crossing, trailed his drogue off the stern, wrecked his rudder
assembly and capsized twice. He might have done better with
a larger drogue off the bow, though it would have put the
spray in his face.

If you trail warps, they should run from cleats abaft the
cockpit and out through a loop near the towing point.

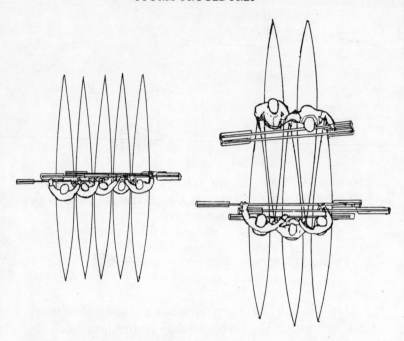

FIG. 8.2 RAFTING UP CANNOT BE RELIED UPON FOR SECURITY IN ROUGH WATER. OF THE TWO METHODS, BOW-TO-COCKPIT IS THE MOST SECURE. SIDE-BY-SIDE RAFTING IS USEFUL FOR RESCUE AID OR TO PROVIDE STABILITY FOR SOME UNUSUAL OPERATION.

RAFTING UP

Rafting up is often taught as a storm procedure, but I do not advise it. It can be a useful manoeuvre for stabilizing a party when some emergency occurs or if you just want everyone to come together for a snack or a discussion of route during moderate conditions. The two most common ways of doing it are to raft the boats cockpit to cockpit or bow to cockpit like sardines. In both cases it is necessary to hold the boats apart at arm's length in choppy water to stop them crunching together

168

and riding up one on the other. Rafting up can stabilize a capsized kayak during re-entry, and it can provide enough stability for sleeping in slender singles during calm weather. It is dangerous, however, to put too much faith in rafting up for stability in heavy weather. Rafting up tends to be the optimist's answer to any emergency, but it can be very strenuous keeping your raft together in high seas, and it turns into an awful mess when you are swatted by an ocean creamer. There are broken paddles, crushed fingers and bleeding people wearing canoes in strange places all over the sea. It is equally dangerous to count on rafting up when you cannot stay awake any longer. What do you do if the waves are too big to make the boats fast bow to cockpit?

Let me repeat what I have said in discussing self-rescue. I believe that to be safe in a sea kayak, you must be capable of surviving alone. The rhyme "less than three shall never be," so reassuring to some, deceptively lulls the inexperienced into believing their ultimate safety relies on clutching onto two companions – but things are just not like that in heavy weather. Then, any boat close enough to touch you is an extreme hazard. A loaded fibreglass kayak carried into you by a breaking wave can cause serious injuries, including concussion and fractured bones. One kayak can be driven right through another – and how do you brace into a breaking wave if there is another kayak on top of yours? By all means paddle with two companions – it is certainly safer – but *don't* base your philosophy of survival on them.

THE ULTIMATE STORMS

Hurricanes – or typhoons, as they are known in Asia and the Pacific – are the ultimate storms: circular monsters anywhere from sixty to a thousand miles across. They, together with their less ferocious cousins the tropical storms, lurk like wolves in the backs of the minds of sailors (and tropical canoeists).

Your first thought must always be to get yourselves and your boats to high ground as fast as possible. Chances are you will have plenty of warning of the approach of such storms (see Chapter 5). The danger of low ground is that a hurricane may cause the level of the sea to rise 15 feet or more. Combine this with giant waves, and you have a sea which will sweep right over the lower atolls and coastal plains. Ideally, you want something like a bomb shelter on a mountaintop to weather it out. Certainly you want some form of substantial protection against wind-blown objects.

I am thankful never to have been caught in a full-fledged hurricane, but when in vulnerable areas my plan and priorities have always been carefully thought out. I frequently cast about me when camped at a new island and think, "Where is the best hurricane shelter around here?" Generally I have decided, if no hurricane-proof dwelling was handy, that I would carry the boats inland to some natural protection such as a rocky outcrop or a thicket of small trees and tie them down. (Larger trees might fall on the boats and smash them.) If such protection were not available, I would dismantle the boats and bury them on high ground.

As the eye of the storm passes over an area, there will be a lull in the wind, then it will start again from the opposite side. Remember when you choose your protection that it must serve from both sides.

SLEEPING IN A KAYAK

The ability and willingness to sleep in the kayak are indispensable to long journeys. Sleeping in the boat is also a necessity for surviving bouts of illness or incapacitation at sea.

The kayak becomes extraordinarily stable when the centre of gravity is lowered, and the lower you can go the better. George Dyson has built kayaks into which he can retreat fully, closing a watertight perspex dome over the cockpit, but it is possible to wriggle down into any high-volume kayak if there is no forward bulkhead and if the bow is not laden with too much gear. (A beam of at least 25 inches is usually required for an average adult.)

Many a kayaker seeking a better mouse-trap has dreamed up a system of inner tubes and paddles to stabilize his craft, but this is not the solution. A beamy kayak with the weight kept low is extremely stable. It will *slide* when hit by a wave. Lindemann used an inner-tube outrigger on his Atlantic crossing and capsized twice *because* of it. His boat would slide until the outrigger dived, at which point the kayak would trip on the outrigger. Romer crossed the same ocean without an outrigger and did not capsize until, on the last leg of his journey, between Puerto Rico and the mainland United States, he was struck and killed by a hurricane. (It was the third hurricane he had met in the course of his voyage, but also the largest. And in Puerto Rico he had destroyed the balance of his boat by adding an outboard motor.)

I have slept slouched down in a kayak on many occasions, and have ridden through gales in such a posture; this is not the greatest way to spend the night but not the worst, either.

SEPARATION AT SEA

Once you have agreed you are going to travel as a group, no one should leave that group unless everybody knows about it and an arrangement is made to link up again. During bad weather, it is important not to spread the party too thinly. Not only will you be slow to give assistance if needed, but you may lose sight of a member who pauses to make repairs or re-adjust gear. In a party with three boats or more, leave a strong paddler to take up the rear if there is doubt about any of the members being able to handle the conditions. It is the lead boat's responsibility to see no one is left behind. This is because a delay up front automatically draws the group together while one astern spreads the party.

Surprisingly, it is often fine, calm weather which causes separations at sea. Everyone is relaxed and confident that nothing could possibly go wrong on such a fine day – "So let's not wait for those turkeys in the other boat. We'll go on and wait on the island." Then of course there is a misunderstanding about which island, or the following boat gets into some sort of unforeseeable trouble and is delayed or obliged to alter course. Once our kayak, which was travelling second on an 8-mile crossing of the Magellan Strait under miraculously calm conditions, was attacked by a wounded seal. The animal bit through the hull in eleven places and we scurried for a rock a couple of miles distant while the other boat continued unaware of the drama, its occupants never suspecting that anything could possibly have gone wrong, and probably irritated by our abrupt change of course. It was two weeks before we were again able to make contact. There was, naturally, a misunderstanding as to the rendezvous point, and it is no simple matter locating a solitary kayak in the midst of such a peppering of wilderness islands.

Separations at sea can usually be avoided by following these guidelines:

1 Make it clearly the responsibility of the lead boat to see that everyone stays within communicating distance.

2 Everyone in the group must hold the same course as the lead boat and nobody is to strike off alone. If you disagree with the course set by the lead boat, discuss it. If you can't agree, establish a rendezvous point.

3 Establish a rendezvous point each day. Normally this will be your lunch stop or the spot where you expect to camp that night. As an extra safeguard, you might agree also on a more distant, back-up rendezvous point, or on the emergency principle of a return to the last camp at which you were all together. The first option is preferable since it won't involve backtracking. It can be very difficult to hunt for a kayak on a rough sea, even from a cliff-top with binoculars. If you are carrying VHF radios, then your chances of prolonged separation are greatly reduced – but only if you have an agreed listening time. This might be, for instance, five minutes each side of the hour.

TOWING

In an emergency such as illness, exhaustion, accident or hypothermia, the best solution may be to tow the incapacitated boat. Towing is also an emergency measure to keep together two boats in which one crew is paddling more weakly than another.

The towing point of a double kayak is immediately abaft the rear cockpit; that of most singles is about a foot astern the

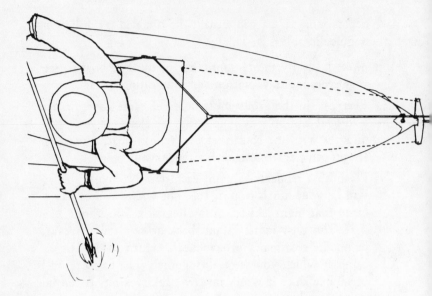

cockpit. A bridle attached to cleats each side of the cockpit, or looped around the lip of the coaming if you have a fibreglass boat with a small cockpit, will provide secure attachment.

A simple system is to pass the rigged drogue from the boat about to be towed across to the towing boat. It is delivered to the No. 2 paddler, who ties it off to the cleats each side of the coaming and tucks the canopy away under the shock cord on deck. This places the drogue swivel neatly over the towing point. It is handy to have a resilient support such as a short whip aerial just above the rudder. (The Klepper conveniently comes with one – wistfully provided by the manufacturer for flying the company pennant!) Just put a clove hitch in the towline and drop it over the aerial. This prevents it fouling the rudder assembly.

Unfortunately, kayaks don't usually tow very well. They tend to yaw badly and must be steered carefully in the wake of

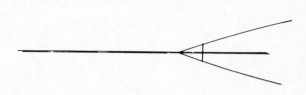

FIG. 8.3 THE IDEAL TOWING POINT ON MOST KAYAKS IS USUALLY SOMEWHERE NEAR THE MIDDLE OF THE AFTER-DECK. IF YOUR BOAT IS FITTED WITH A RUDDER, A TOWING POST IS NECESSARY TO KEEP THE TOWLINE FROM DAMAGING THE RUDDER ASSEMBLY.

the towing boat. This can prove a problem in a single if the canoeist is incapacitated. If the cripple is in one of the less stable boats, a third kayak will be needed to prop him up, so the formula is complicated even more – your one strong boat will be towing two kayaks. Ideally, you should have at least one double kayak in every party so you can transfer a sick person into its forward cockpit. A strong paddler can paddle a double alone and still average two knots under neutral conditions. Once when I was injured, my petite wife paddled a fully loaded Klepper 10 miles in four hours with me as an inert lump in the passenger seat. Next day, a companion paddled me the last 14 miles to hospital. I shudder to think what we would have done if we had all been in singles, since I had a sky-high temperature and an infection which would soon have required amputation of the arm.

9
Camping & Food Gathering

Some folks carry the most imaginative gadgetry to make camping easier, but the wilderness has a healthy knack of trimming these extras so that by the end of the second month, you will be reduced to the most basic equipment. Chances are, by the end of a long trip, if the weather has been tolerable you won't have used your primus for ages, having realized you could light a fire almost as quickly and that the fire was a lot more friendly. Your pressure cooker will become an ordinary cooking pot, since you won't have to worry about fuel shortages once you begin to use firewood. (Obviously, where wood is becoming scarce it is better to use the stove.) And as for cooking time, what does fifteen minutes matter away from the hustle of city life? (It is another matter altogether, of course, if you are rationing fuel.) Your knife, fork, spoon, cup and plates will probably be reduced to a spoon, a bowl and a jack-knife. The dinky little hatchet you started out with will have been traded for a three-pound long-handled axe. Who knows, you might abandon the tent altogether and carry only a waterproof fly and groundsheet like the native hunters.

CAMPING IN THE LAND OF STORMS

Selecting the best campsite from the sea is an important first step. In British Columbia or Patagonia you know you are doing it right when you start finding the remains of old Indian camps as you clear the ground for your tent. The chart will often give a good indication of the most favourable sort of place for a landing. According to preference, you might select a sheltered cove or fjord close to the jumping-off point for the next day or go in behind a headland which offers a better view of the seas outside. The head of a larger bay will usually have a stream, better shelter and easier landing. Beware of landing on an exposed coast during moderate surf when there is a likelihood of deteriorating weather which could prevent your getting off next morning. Streams large enough to appear on your chart may well offer a protected path to shore, and of course a supply of clean fresh water. If you plan to camp for a day or two at the one site, choose a location with plenty of firewood. In Patagonia, this means looking for stands of tepu or cypress. Tepu, a feathery leafed tree common along the shores, is such good firewood that it will burn green. Cypress too is excellent. On once occasion I pulled a pole of cypress from a bog where it may well have lain for fifty years. Once it was split it burned fiercely. In Alaska or British Columbia look for a windfall cedar or for a beach piled high with driftwood.

If you are travelling double or in a group, you will develop a routine. Try to make it a good one. For instance, as soon as you land one person can take the tent and primus (if you are still using primuses) and billy to the selected site and put on water for a brew, then pitch the tent and loft the bags while another person unloads and cares for the boats. Whether you use a fire or a primus, it pays to get it going without loss of time since if someone is cold, the warm drink is cheering and the activity of making a fire and a meal is good for morale. The first fifteen minutes after you clamber out of the kayak on a miserable day is the easiest time to catch yourself an incapacitating chill.

If firewood is plentiful, build a good-sized fire. The initial blaze will boil the water quickly and the resulting coals can be used to cook the main meal, with a pile of driftwood and dead timber collected ready to throw on as soon as the meal is cooked. During bad weather, a lightweight canvas fly erected well above the fire protects it from rain. Nylon is no good for this purpose since sparks quickly ventilate it.

Starting a fire in the rain has probably occupied more pages of boy-scout manuals than anything else. My own solution is to carry an old rubber inner tube. A few square inches of this can easily be lit and set in the midst of small twigs – gathered from the underside of some fallen tree or split from the centre of a dry cypress pole. The flaming molten rubber quickly establishes the heart of the fire, if you have selected a site sheltered from the wind.

Contrary to popular belief, a kayaker *can* usually find a sheltered campsite on stormy coasts. Although you can expect to need a storm tent (and occasionally you will be glad of it), you can get by with a waterproof 10-foot by 12-foot tarpaulin pitched well into the trees and a sheet of plastic on the ground. Nylon is good for the fly, but it is very vulnerable to sparks from the fire.

Mice and rats are frequently a problem. Sometimes islands are overrun with them, and if you camp in old dwellings you are bound to meet the resident rodents. In Chile I once had fifteen holes eaten in the buoyancy tubing of my boat; it seems they just fancied plastic, and from then on my equipment included a sturdy rat trap.

In British Columbia and Alaska, bears, especially the grizzly, can also pose a problem for camping kayakers. Camping at river mouths in August when the salmon are running is a particularly reliable way of getting into trouble. Woe betide the hapless kayaker who pitches his tent by a happy bear's exclusive fishing hole or beaches his boat on the bear's buried food supply. Climb a tree if you must. Grizzlies, unlike blacks, are restricted to the ground.

Hungry bears are more difficult to avoid than full ones. Members of the Washington Kayak Club had their camp raided by black bears on their 1980 summer expedition. They found the bears were far better at climbing trees than they themselves, and that the trees were too close together to rig a safe food cache. Eventually they anchored a kayak offshore with their food supply in it and drove the bears off with much yelling and stone-throwing. (The same trick tried by inland kayakers on the Bowron Lakes a few years ago was less successful. The bears swam out to the boats, wrecking kayaks, cameras and other gear as they helped themselves to the tastier items in the cache.)

Jim Allan, of Ecosummer Canada Expeditions Ltd., an authority on bears, uses a different technique. He carries a piece of ripe pepperoni sausage and ties it tantalizingly out of reach of the bears, well away from camp. "They'll fart around that all night," he says.

The other main risk is simply surprising a bear – or worse, surprising a mother with her cubs. Ashore, travel with a noisemaker: a clanking sierra cup or a chatterbox companion. If you do meet a bear, back off carefully. The only serviceable active defense is a heavy-gauge shotgun at very close range (no more than fifteen feet). If you *are* attacked, your last resort is to play dead and hope the fantasy doesn't come true.

CAMPING IN THE SUN

Life is easier in the tropics, but camping has its own special problems. Shade is a priority, and you have to consider insects (especially if you are near a swamp), breeze and water supply.

Tropical rivers are more contaminated than those in cold climates and you must regard pools of water with great suspicion. All but rainwater should be boiled or treated with purifying tablets.

Coconut plantations make great campsites, but watch out for falling coconuts – and that is no joke: a 10-lb coconut falling 20 or 30 feet is quite capable of killing you. Your cooking fire and tent should be well clear of delicately poised coconuts and loosely hanging fronds. If you must camp beneath a coconut palm, first pull off all dead fronds and knock down threatening coconuts. Of course, you may have some trouble convincing the plantation owner that the coconut threatened you first, so it is well to befriend him beforehand.

Coconut plantations also provide an abundance of old dried coconuts for campfires, and the dried flowerstalks and fronds burn very well. If the plantation has been frequently worked there may be piles of discarded dry husks left by the copra gatherers. These make excellent fuel. The young coconuts are a source of fine sweet water and the older ones of a nutritious white flesh. Sharing your tropical garden of Eden you may find a population of large, edible crabs, either the tree climbing variety or the burrowing land crabs. Unfortunately, coconut plantations are also host to mosquitoes and a variety of sandflies which may breed in the old coconut husks and down the burrows of land crabs. It is advisable to have a fine mesh mosquito net since some sandflies are so minute as to be almost invisible. A tent with a netted entrance is well worth carrying, as is an insect repellant.

The problem with camping in a mangrove swamp is that the tide usually floods your campsite twice a day. Assuming there is no high ground, this leaves you two choices: sleep in the trees or sleep in the boat.

The best way to sleep in the trees is with a hammock. A

good one is the U.S. military jungle hammock with sewn-in roof and mosquito netting. Take care to sleep on a layer of blanket as well as covering yourself, since mosquitoes are capable of biting into your back through the tight fabric.

If the mangroves are too small for a hammock, you will have to turn your boat into a bed, and your comfort is going to depend to a large extent on the type of craft you have. If you come in to the swamp at high tide, take care you have not moored your canoe above a stake or submerged branch. Hang the gear in the upper branches to give you space, then inflate your air mattress and rig a mosquito net from the thinnest nearby branches. Mosquitoes can be particularly bad in mangrove swamps near river or stream entrances.

SECURITY

When camping in populated areas where you fear malicious behaviour or theft from the locals, you must give some thought to security. The following points should be considered for protection against sneak thieves:

1 Pitch the tents within easy earshot and with the entrances facing each other.

2 Put the boats in the midst of the camp so they are visible from every tent. You might also make the tents fast to a cleat on the coaming.

3 Take valuables into the tents and store them between the occupants or under your pillows. Put the remainder of your gear inside the boats with the spray skirts tied off.

4 If you must, stretch a fishing line tight around camp at a height of four inches. Attach it to a precariously

balanced pot of cutlery which will crash down when the line is tripped.

5 Keep a pack of mini-flares and a powerful flashlight handy. A dazzling light can be most intimidating, as can a flare fired aloft. Mini-flares are dangerous firearms and should not be pointed at prowlers unless life is threatened.

6 Don't leave axes, machetes, spear guns or knives lying around camp at night; slip them under your tent or boat so *you* know where they are.

FOOD

There has been a great deal written about food and diet on expeditions, and a canoe trip is little different from any other strenuous journey. You can expect to burn up a tremendous number of calories. It is most important to maintain this energy supply. No matter what you eat, you will feel great lethargy and weariness during the early days of constant paddling, but an inadequate diet will make things a lot worse. In cold climates, the problem of energy supply becomes even more serious since so many calories are burned up just keeping warm.

The critical point in making the adaptation from the easy life most people lead to that demanded by the rigours of a long kayak trip is the availability of energy from the food. A body that is accustomed to extracting its energy from a readily available source such as sugar or starch will become starved as it struggles to cope with a protein diet. When it can no longer get its energy from one source, it moves on to the next, but the breaking down of protein into energy is so slow that at first the body cannot keep up.

During the first three weeks of the 1973–74 Chilean Kayak Expedition, we developed an insatiable craving for carbohydrate. The hunting was excellent and we could eat the lean steamer ducks to the tune of five pounds of meat each per day and still feel hungry, though our stomachs could contain no more food. It was not until we were able to purchase forty-eight cans of sweetened condensed milk, which we quaffed at the rate of one can per person per day, that we began to recover from this strange form of starvation. Sweets and plenty of sweet drinks are not luxuries; they are necessities for most people. Good food and time to let your body consume it are necessary if you are not going to burn yourself up on a long trip. The ideal is to eat as you did at home: three hearty meals a day, and then sleep for eight hours every night – but that is just not sea canoeing. More likely you will paddle twelve hours or more on a handful of raisins and a couple of buns with bully beef. You may do a lot worse than that, gradually drawing ever more heavily on your body's reserves. My suggestion for long wilderness trips is to carry only fats, milk powder, sugar, spices and carbohydrates (rice, flour, etc.) and rely on nature for the protein. You should always, however, carry a small supply of emergency freeze-dried protein.

The best food for paddling is something with little bulk and high energy content. Raisins are good, as are almonds or walnuts. Peanuts and cashews are reportedly more difficult to digest. Sweetened condensed milk is an excellent energy food which carries well until it is opened. Chocolate is a great standby, and I usually like to eat some bread, with either bully beef or canned sardines, taking care to drink all the oil. Strenuous paddling discourages large meals since hardworking stomach muscles just won't cope well with a full belly. Leave your main meals till you get ashore. Interestingly, Lindemann, who is a physician as well as a German, carried one can of beer per day on his trans-Atlantic crossing.

HUNTING, FISHING AND DIVING FROM A KAYAK

The kayak was originally developed by the Eskimos for hunting seal, walrus, caribou and even whales. It is silent, unobtrusive and swift, and you may hunt from it using rifle, shotgun, spear or bow and arrow. In New Zealand the boats have even been used for hunting commercially. It is, however, difficult to shoot accurately while seated in a kayak if there is any wave action at all, and on the sea, of course, there usually is. One technique is to swing the rifle freely across the target, squeezing the trigger in brief anticipation of lining up. Plenty of practice with an air rifle is desirable before you start using a rifle with expensive ammunition.

Probably the best all-purpose survival rifle for a kayak expedition is the AR-7 .22 semi-automatic, which folds away inside its own butt, floats, resists corrosion and is quite accurate. You can carry a thousand rounds of ammunition in the same volume as fifty shotgun shells. For Arctic paddling, however, a heavier calibre rifle is desirable, since there is the possibility of having to deal with polar bear or walrus.

The normal cruising speed of a kayak is just about right for successful trolling, though it may be a little slow for some species of fish. If you use a sturdy hand-line – say about 80–lb test monofilament nylon with a stainless steel leader of 35–lb test-you will have a line you can manage, yet one that will let off anything too big for you to handle. In barracuda country, it means losing a lot of lures, but you don't really want to share your kayak with a barracuda capable of breaking a 35–lb leader. A hand reel or a rod can be worked well from a kayak, giving you control of the line without cutting your fingers. A short-handled gaff with a wrist thong may also prove useful to bring your catch aboard if you plan to do a lot of fishing. Keep a cloth sack handy for carrying fish on deck.

A kayak is not the ideal craft from which to dive, but kayaking and diving nevertheless frequently go together; certainly, diving equipment can prove very handy during an emergency involving kayaks. Two divers can operate from a double kayak, but it is usually best for only one to be in the water at a time, the other waiting in the boat, ready to receive a fish off the spear or to give assistance. A good free diver can fish comfortably in 40 feet of water and with practice can go twice that deep. If you happen to have access to scuba, the tanks can be carried to the dive site on the after-deck (in a calm sea) and put on either while sitting on the rear of the cockpit or as soon as you are in the water, where they can be held by slings. A diver should of course avoid carrying speared fish in the hand when there may be sharks in the vicinity. When diving on the drop-off of a large coral reef, use the kayak to cross the wide, sandy shallows, which can often go a half mile or more. The canoe can then be tied off to a coral head inside the calm while the divers swim out through cuts in the reef to deeper water.

IO
First Aid

This chapter, like the chapter on navigation and the section devoted to tides, is intended to supplement knowledge the reader may already have or which he can gain from other sources. In this case, I assume that the reader will have some practical knowledge of standard first-aid skills. Basic instructions such as the treatment of wounds, fractures and burns, mouth-to-mouth resuscitation, external cardiac massage and treatment of shock are therefore omitted from the following discussion.

Ideally, you should try to include someone with practical medical experience in your party. Expeditions, however, may require ordinary members to administer treatment beyond the limits of normal first aid, and it is advisable to carry with you an advanced manual of medical emergency practice. A good choice is *Medicine for Mountaineering*, edited by James A. Wilkerson, M.D.

The following is an outline of some special medical problems a kayak expedition is likely to meet.

TENOSYNOVITIS

This is a painful inflammation of the tendons in the wrist and arm. It is most common in the wrist and arm that twist the feathered paddle.

PREVENTION: Use unfeathered paddles. Work up gradually to distance paddling.

TREATMENT: Some relief may be gained from firm bandaging, but the only sure cure is a few days' rest.

CANOEIST'S ARM

This may be just a more advanced form of tenosynovitis. It is a creeping numbness which begins in the fingers and sometimes works its way up the hand, wrist and arm to the shoulders. In chronic cases the canoeist will not be able to hold the paddle. It is probably a result of long-term damage from the use of feathered paddles, since only the arm which twists the paddle is affected. The damage appears to be long lasting.

PREVENTION: Use unfeathered paddles.

CHAFING AND SALT WATER RASHES

These mostly occur under the arms and where the body touches the coaming, spray skirts and backrest. They may be very painful and on long crossings may develop to the point of bleeding. When leaving the beach through surf, wave splashes can also sometimes carry sand up your trouser legs. This sand can be badly irritating if you then have to sit on it for a day or more.

PREVENTION: Rub susceptible places with coconut oil before departure. A liberal coat over the whole upper torso provides effective protection for eight hours. Wash the sand out of your pants if necessary after launching through surf.

TREATMENT: Rest ashore with frequent freshwater washes. Avoid sweating, or swimming in the sea. Tape and bandages will ease the discomfort till land is reached.

BOILS AND CARBUNCLES

Lindemann was badly affected by these during his Atlantic crossing of 1956, and the problem has afflicted many other sea kayakers with whom I have corresponded. Some people react to the salt, the chafing, and the drastic change of bodily routine that expeditions demand by developing these painful skin infections on arms, backs, buttocks and thighs.

TREATMENT: Boils can be treated either individually as they occur, with a sulfur-based powder after being brought to a head with a poultice, or as a last resort, when the infection looks as if it is becoming dangerous, with antibiotics either by injection or in tablet form. Antibiotic cream can be very effective once the wound has been cleansed. Should the boil fail to respond to treatment and the infection become angrier, get the patient to a doctor quickly. More serious infection can readily set in, particularly in the tropics.

BLISTERS

These are usually worst near the start of the trip. It is better to tape your hands extensively before setting off than to patch the holes at mid-day. Paddling in hot humid weather causes more blisters than cold weather canoeing. If a fluid-filled blister develops, avoid breaking the skin if possible. Don't attempt to pop it with a needle.

SEASICKNESS

I have several times been badly seasick in a kayak myself, and as anyone who has suffered the problem knows, it is a grim experience. In a kayak there is little you can do except grit your teeth and keep paddling.

PREVENTION: Seasickness can be prevented with a variety of tablets, the best of which I have found to be Bonine. These tablets should be taken one hour before entering rough water, and are good for about twelve hours. Caffein may be needed to counter any drowsiness the tablets may cause.

TREATMENT: Anti-emetic suppositories can be used to prevent otherwise uncontrollable dry-retching. If possible, a period of rest should be taken since the action of paddling aggravates an upset stomach. Try to eat bland, non-acidic foods and build up your water intake gradually. A bad case of seasickness must be treated seriously in the tropics where dehydration and the resulting hyperthermia (overheating) endanger life.

KAYAKER'S ELBOW

This is tennis elbow by another name: a painful swelling which occurs on an elbow strained by too much paddling. It is similar in nature to "water on the knee" and requires a week of rest with the arm out of action. The elbow and nearby tissue become very sensitive, and the healing of wounds or infection in the area is inhibited because of the impaired blood supply through the fluid-bloated tissue. This affliction is painful and will demand to be treated as the serious injury which it is.

SUNBURN

The potential for injury by this means on the open sea in a kayak is catastrophic.

PREVENTION: In tropical regions, begin with careful exposure to the hot sun. A wide-brimmed hat and long-sleeved cotton shirt can be removed occasionally to allow a gradual tanning which will give you natural protection against sunburn. Many doctors may disagree with tanning on the grounds of an increased risk of skin cancer, but the tan can prove a survival asset in an emergency. It certainly makes living ashore in the tropics a good deal easier. For fair-haired people, the protection required includes a good hat, a bandit's mask to cover nose and lips, a long-sleeved shirt with a high collar, protective flaps or bandages for the backs of hands and wrists, and zinc cream for any areas that must be left exposed. You have a choice between looking like an Egyptian mummy or a boiled lobster. Take the mummy.

TREATMENT: If serious sunburning does occur, the skin may blister and the victim dehydrate even to the point of delirium. The patient should be taken to hospital if the burning is that extensive. If this is not possible, you will have to camp and treat the burns yourself:

1 Be sure the patient drinks plenty of water.
2 Don't break any blisters, since they will be prone to infection.
3 Cool the patient with sponge baths of clean seawater.
4 Avoid the use of burn creams on open skin.
5 Keep the patient well clear of the sun for several days after the burn has begun to recover.

INFECTIONS

Sea kayaking expeditions may force great changes on the body: new and strenuous exercises, irregular sleep routines, strange foods, different temperatures and a whole new variety of bacteria against which your body will have to develop fresh immunity. It is not surprising, then, that on expeditions the body appears to have less resistance to infection than normal. Add to this the stress factor from anxiety or interpersonal emotional stress and you can lower resistance to infection later in the trip. This is particularly so in the tropics, where your expedition medic can expect plenty of infected wounds, sores, bites, ears, eyes, etc. Many will be manageable with topical creams, but you should be well stocked with a wide range of antibiotics in both tablet and injection form.

Kidney infections in particular are regrettably common on long-distance canoe trips. Doctors to whom I have spoken about this tend to agree that prolonged periods seated in a kayak can retard the functioning of the kidneys and increase the likelihood of serious renal infection. Symptoms include pain and aching in the region of the kidneys and urinal tract, painful and difficult urination, discharge in urine, and fever. Should this occur when you are unable to reach a hospital, you should treat with a specific course of an antibiotic. Ensure that the patient drinks plenty of fluids.

HYPERTHERMIA

Hyperthermia is the overheating of the body usually as a result of insufficient fluid intake, combined with hot, still conditions. It can also be the result of a high fever or being overdressed and overworked in hot climates. It is a common hazard for kayakers in the tropics. Symptoms are an inability to cool the body, an excessively high body temperature, breathlessness, dry mouth, dizzy spells, affected vision, headaches, poor concentration and eventually delirium, unconsciousness and death.

TREATMENT: Give the patient plenty of water. Keep clothing wet and give plenty of cool sponge baths, particularly to the head, neck and wrists. At sea, wet the patient's hat frequently to cool the head, and have him wear a wet neck bandanna. Trail the patient's hands in the water frequently and if the temperature won't come down, put him over the side for a swim. Avoid paddling during the heat of day if it is reasonable to do so.

DEHYDRATION

The risk of dehydration is acute in the tropics. I advocate carrying five gallons of water per double, and suggest that any expedition that may face water supply problems carry both a hand-operated desalination unit and the means to distill seawater from a fire on shore. Some people require considerably more water than others and though one obviously must conserve water where it is scarce, it is important that all canoeists drink the amount they need. Survival manuals usually suggest one pint per person per day as an absolute minimum. Learn the needs of all members of your group and keep plenty of water handy during the day. A symptom of dehydration is abnormally dark urine.

HALLUCINATIONS

Hallucinating as a result of fatigue and long hours of wakefulness is quite normal and should not be a cause for panic. You are not going mad; all you need is some sleep. Hallucinations occur more readily at night, sometimes after as little as twenty hours awake. They are just like dreams which intrude on your consciousness. Once you are visited by them, you can safely afford to continue paddling for only a limited time. If you begin hallucinating at 4:00 A.M., you will probably be able to continue until dawn, when daylight greatly reduces the symptoms, but if you begin your fantastic visions early in the night, you will usually have to take some sleep before you next see the sun. Strong coffee has some temporary countering effects. Common visions include feeling the presence of nonexistent canoeists and visions of land, trees, lights, and the like. Maintaining an accurate course ultimately becomes a hopeless task, and it is better to get sleep *before* you become too unreliable.

HYPOTHERMIA

Hypothermia, or exposure, is probably responsible directly or indirectly for more accidental kayaking deaths than all other factors combined. Though death by drowning may be the coroner's verdict, the cause of drowning is frequently hypothermia. Because it is the number one killer, it is vital that it be thoroughly understood and that appropriate precautions be taken when paddling in cold climates.

Hypothermia is a drop in the body's core temperature below the critical level of 32° to 33°C (90°F). Once body temperature reaches this level, unconsciousness usually supervenes. When the temperature reaches 30°C (85°F), a victim who has not already drowned through unconsciousness or loss of dexterity will die by means of heart failure.

Susceptibility to hypothermia depends not only on the conditions of exposure but also on body size. Children are considerably more susceptible than large adults, and thin people more susceptible than the fat. The warning signs of hypothermia, in approximate sequence of severity, are:

1 Uncontrollable shivering and an apparent inability to warm up;
2 Despair and disinterest;
3 Erratic paddling and an inability to maintain course;
4 Blurred vision and lack of coordination;
5 Ashen face and hands;
6 Muscle rigidity, replacing the previous shivering;
7 Incoherence and collapse.

Sometimes a person on the verge of hypothermia will recognize in himself such early signs as uncontrollable shivering and blurred vision. If you find yourself in such a fix, you should immediately seek warmth and warn your companions of your condition. It is not safe, however, to rely on members of your party recognizing the onset of hypothermia in themselves. In cold conditions, always keep watch for the symptoms in other members as well as in yourself. Remember too that there is an established link between despair and hypothermia. People without hope are more prone to hypothermia, and those whose morale has sagged should be watched carefully for additional warning signs.

PREVENTION: If you are making a night crossing with wind and rain, have wool clothes and windproofs. Don't wait until you are already shuddering to put on your windproofs. Try to *maintain* your warmth, rather than lose and regain it. Eat well before setting out on a cold crossing. After a day of hungry paddling, eat well and eat soon – especially if you are in for a cold, miserable night. Wear a hat in the cold. If you are likely to be in for an icy swim, wear an immersion suit with a hood, or a wetsuit with a hood.

If you *do* find yourself in cold water without the protection of an immersion suit or your boat, the outlook is grim. Thrashing around will bring your temperature down fast. Treading water will cool you into unconsciousness almost twice as fast as holding still. Swimming will only kill you unless the land is *very* close. Depending on the temperature of the water, you may be able to swim ten yards or you might get half a mile. If help is to be had, you can increase your chances by waiting for it quietly. If you have your life jacket, inflate it and hang in the fetal position. If you don't have a life jacket, treading water is better than keeping your head in the drink. The so-called "drownproofing" technique, which involves hanging with your head underwater between breaths, may be fine in a warm swimming pool. In a cold sea it is suicide. It may be stating the obvious, but get out of the water and into the boat again as fast as you can.

TREATMENT: If someone in your party develops advanced symptoms of hypothermia you must deal with the problem at once. The victim must always be treated as a stretcher case. That means he does no more paddling. The victim should be dressed as warmly as possible and should ride as a passenger in a double. If you are in singles, he will have to be towed.

Carry the victim as gently as possible (preferably in the kayak) to shelter, and remove his clothing so that heat – from whatever source is available – can reach his body more easily. The normal field procedure is for one or two other members of the party to strip and join the victim in a dry sleeping bag in order to warm him. In the meantime, water should be heated.

The latest recommendation from the U.S. Coast Guard, based on recent research at the University of Victoria and elsewhere, is that pieces of clothing soaked in warm (not scalding) water should then be applied to the victim's head, neck, sides, chest and groin, and these warm compresses should be changed as often as required in order to continue gently warming him.

Note: Stimulation of any kind – through physical exercise, jostling, rubbing the limbs, or the administration of alcohol or hot drinks – should be avoided. Do *not* give the victim a warm drink until his body temperature has returned to the vicinity of normal. A hot drink can draw warm blood away from the vital organs where it is most needed, and physical activity can bring cold, stagnant blood from the extremities to the body core, killing a victim who has already begun to recover.

Remember that it is useless to wrap a victim of hypothermia in a cold blanket or sleeping bag. Once his core temperature has dropped below the critical level, he is no longer generating sufficient body heat to get warm of his own accord. Insulation alone will do him no good. Insulation and a gentle source of heat are required.

An improvised fire still

II
Survival Situations

The key to survival at sea is to think survival long before the event. Like the boy scout, *be prepared*. If you become a castaway, thinking survival means wasting nothing; potentially useful equipment must always be kept since it may contain a wire or a nail which will save your life. Thinking survival means always carrying essential articles in the pockets of your immersion suit or anorak – waterproof matches, a knife, a space blanket, fishing line, hooks and a mirror (heliograph) so if you make it to shore without your boat, you will have the means to improve your chances of survival. Thinking survival means taking precautions like tying up your boat on windy days even if it is pulled clear of the water. I once watched a gust of wind pick up my partially loaded kayak and smash it down a hundred yards away. Such a wind could as well have carried it out to sea – with disastrous results if I had been on a wilderness island. Thinking survival means not throwing away your gumboots if you have to swim to shore; if you must take them off (your life jacket should keep you afloat), hold them under your armpits. Filled with air they will provide buoyancy for your swim, and you will have boots to protect your feet from the rocks when you arrive. Cold weather survival preparation means having the right thermal equipment, but it also involves getting your body ready for hardship by deliberately underdressing and swimming frequently in cold water. This may sound masochistic, but it does increase your resistance to cold.

The Ona Indians of Tierra del Fuego wore almost no clothes even under snowy conditions. They were apparently no different from us physiologically, but they had developed extraordinary resistance to cold. Once upon a time they caught a zealous missionary and decided he was worth converting. The first stage demanded relieving him of his smelly clothes and plucking all his unsightly bodily hair. For six months that missionary lived naked on Tierra del Fuego before being rescued by a passing ship, and at the time of his rescue he was in excellent health. It is a good story to remember when you start to think cold weather survival. The missionary would have had shelter, a fire and food – all of which no doubt contributed significantly to his survival – but most important, his body adapted to life in the cold.

You don't have to be on some mighty expedition to get yourself into a sea-survival crisis (though it certainly helps). You are in one of these crises as soon as you are in the water unable to get back into your boat. The main difference between being in the harbour or being in the middle of the ocean is your chance of getting outside help.

SURVIVAL AT SEA WITH NO BOAT

Your survival in the water is going to depend on how much warning you had of the emergency, and on what survival equipment is available to you.

If you have no special clothing to protect you, your chances of surviving in temperatures below 10°C for longer than an hour are slim indeed. Your best chance is to wear a survival or immersion suit with warm underclothing. Next best is a wetsuit (the more complete the better); next best again an exposure jacket (floater coat) with a sea-seat to keep you out of the water, and next best again a survival bag along with all the clothing you can wear. The clothing will hold a considerable amount of body-warmed water, and the exposure bag will further slow down its loss. You should have a neoprene hood or woolly hat to cover your head and neck, since this is the region from which the body loses heat most rapidly. The armpits and crotch are other areas of rapid heat loss. If you have only a life jacket, hunch your body into a tight ball and hang in the water, moving as little as possible. If there are several of you, form a huddle to share your warmth (this can double the time you survive).

SURVIVAL WITH A BOAT

Expedition canoeists will normally have with them all they need to survive. The main danger is that they will squander strength and energy, abandoning mental resourcefulness through panicky behaviour. As soon as you realize you are lost or unable to reach the land you desire,

1 Get out the chart and examine every possibility and factor affecting you, then decide on the best course of action and keep to it. Consider it a maxim in these situations that the group must always stay together.

2 Since this course may involve days of open sea canoeing before you reach land, ration water and food immediately and see that everyone in the group understands your predicament fully.

3 In the tropics, paddle by night and conserve your strength during the heat of the day when you can use the solar stills or desalination pumps to collect fresh water. Build a rainwater catchment system ready for instant use and keep it clear of the sea salt. Rig a sail if

this is consistent with your direction of travel. Do whatever you can to save effort.

4 If you require assistance, turn on the emergency locator beacon and watch for aircraft and ships. One person should always remain on watch when the group is sleeping, just in case a ship should appear.

5 If you are in cold conditions, dress warmly.

6 Start gathering seafood. A fishing line should be trolled and a spear kept at hand. You may catch dorado, jacks, tuna, turtles or any of many varieties of school fish. Very small sharks may be caught or speared from the boat, but don't spear anything too big. The only bird a canoeist could hope to catch for food is probably the ever-curious booby, which is naive enough to think people are harmless. These will often come close to you, even attempting to land on the tips of paddles and attractive hats.

Dougal Robertson, author of *Survive the Savage Sea*, and an excellent manual called *Sea Survival*, which should be mandatory reading for all sea canoeists, describes the capture and use of turtles for survival. Their blood can be drunk to quench thirst and their meat eaten dried, cooked (if you have a primus) or raw.

"Survival-think" requires intense concentration on the problems involved with gathering water, feeding, protecting the group and keeping together. You must be prepared to spend the longest likely time on the sea and not develop a rescue-dependent mentality which will only lead to despair when ships or land fail to appear. The morale of the group is most important during such a crisis. Those who fully understand the position should explain it clearly to those who are doubting the course of action. A group whose morale is low, be it through navigational uncertainty or because they have given up hope of ever seeing land again, is a group that is more susceptible to mental collapse and consequent ailments such as hypothermia.

DRINKING WATER

After air, fresh water is your most valuable commodity. In the tropics your need will be greater than in the temperate zone since your water loss will be higher. Prevention of water loss and collection of fresh supplies therefore should become a priority as soon as it is obvious you are lost at sea or due for a prolonged crossing. The continuation of bodily functions demands a minimum of one pint of water per person per day, but some people need more than this.

To prevent water loss,

1 Rest during the heat of the day.
2 Wear a hat, and cool yourself off by splashing seawater on your clothing frequently.
3 Treat illnesses such as seasickness and diarrhea as soon as they appear; they waste valuable body fluids and hasten hyperthermia.
4 Avoid filling water bottles completely. Always try to leave enough air in the container so it will float should you drop it overboard.

The methods of water collection at sea, in order of technological sophistication, are these:

1 Rain storms can fill your water containers quickly. A tent fly spread wide on two paddles can do the trick. If

the wind accompanies the rain, however, you may have to devise a smaller catchment. Take care not to collect salt contaminated water into existing freshwater supplies.

2 An RAF survival still is ideal for carrying in a kayak during tropical trips. It folds to the size of a lunch bag and inflates like a large beach ball, consisting as it does of a double inflatable balloon. The inner balloon, of a semi-permeable black material, is partly filled with seawater. Spacers hold it in place within the outer plastic balloon. Heat from the sun causes evaporation from the dark inner bag and condensation on the plastic outer bag where it touches the sea or the surrounding air. The unit contains a tap at the bottom with a plastic bladder for the distilled water. Depending on the size of the still and the strength of the sun, this little gadget may produce as much as a pint of fresh water an hour. It is fragile, however, and will repay rough handling with brackish water.

3 A reverse-osmosis hand-desalination pump will probably cost you more than your kayak, but it could be equally important in keeping you alive. Seagold Industries, Vancouver, B.C., makes an excellent model, about the size of a large grease gun, which will produce fresh water at the rate of a gallon an hour.

MAROONED

Stranded on an uninhabited island may sound like a junior accountant's dream or a philosopher's chance to try out his theories, but it is not so far fetched a possibility, given the sea kayaker's curiosity about the uninhabited and, of course, his means of getting there. You have only to misjudge the surf and break your boat in two, or leave your kayak within reach of the incoming tide, and you are marooned. You may not be as marooned as Robinson Crusoe, but you are going to have to brush up your act. A lot depends on your circumstances, of course. You may just be in for an uncomfortable night before you are missed and a search is mounted, or you may be on an Arctic or tropical island where any mistakes could be fatal. Your chances will also depend on what you were able to salvage from your boat, on what protection you have from the elements, and on the availability of fresh water.

Tropical Survival Ashore

On finding yourself marooned in the tropics, your priorities might be these:

1 See that your partner and other members are safely clear of the sea.

2 Treat any injuries that demand urgent attention.

3 Salvage the boats and any equipment that can be safely reached.

4 Find shelter, and make an assessment of the damage, loss and prospects.

5 See to your water needs. Start rationing water till you know you can get more.

You can survive for weeks without food, but in the tropics few people could survive three days without water. Assuring a supply of water therefore is a priority for tropical castaways. Ashore as at sea, you must take care to prevent water loss by avoiding strenuous exercise during the heat of the day, by doing what you can to cool yourself off, and by treating symptoms such as fever, vomiting and diarrhea which dehydrate the body.

If you are on an island large enough to have streams, your water problems are solved. Swamps too can provide a regular source. Good water can be collected by digging a hole amongst the matted roots of plants near the edge of the swamp. Bail the hole continuously with a cup so inflowing water is filtered through the ground. It is very important that water gained in this way, or from tropical streams, be boiled thoroughly.

On sandy atolls where there is greenery, you will be able to get fresh water by digging to sea level inside the vegetation zone. The water you will find has fallen on the island as rain and been segregated from the seawater by the sand. If the water is brackish, try further inland. One cheeky method is to use the burrows of large land crabs, which frequently reach fresh water. Lower a rubber hose with a cloth filter on the end, link the hose to your boat pump, and suck out the water. You may have such a hose in the form of a spare elastic for your spear gun.

Included in your regular tropical survival equipment should be the makings for a fire still. You need: the camp pressure cooker, six feet of rubber tubing (your spare spear gun rubber), one aluminum tent pole, an 8-foot coil of ⅛-inch copper tubing, some clear plastic surgical tubing, a large bucket (or a rock pool will do) and plenty of water containers. The spear gun rubber should fit snugly over the safety vent on top of the pressure cooker as well as over the end of the copper tubing. It should also fit inside the tent pole. The whole unit is assembled as shown in the photograph on page 198. You can use a waterproof Klepper bag as a cooling tank. It will have to be constantly refilled with cool water from the sea, because the condenser heats it up quickly.

Maintain the seawater level in the pressure cooker and scour the inside every four or five hours. Otherwise, you may find some pretty acrid tastes contaminating your new water supply. This is a very reliable method for getting fresh water and, though it demands constant surveillance, it will produce a gallon of good water every two hours.

Once your supply of water is assured and you have shelter from the sun and the rain and wind, you will probably spend all your energy gathering and preparing food as well as perfecting your efforts to attract the attention of would-be rescuers.

The sea is a vast larder for the tropical wilderness canoeist or the castaway. At low tide, shellfish can be gathered from rocks or coral reefs and an amazing variety of pool fish caught with a stick. Crayfish and crabs can often be nabbed in quite shallow water, and the pools may contain small octopus as well as shrimp, sea cucumbers and sea urchins. You may, however, encounter naturally contaminated sea creatures in the Leeward Islands and certain other Caribbean zones where a mysterious fish poisoning makes the taking of fish a risky business. World-wide there is also the occasional danger of red-tide poisoning. If in doubt, it seems safest to stick to filter feeders (scallops, oysters, mussels and the like) and to small species of carnivorous fish where there is danger of tropical poisoning, and to avoid precisely these species where there is danger of red tide.

Bottom fishing with a hand line is efficient if you can reach deep water without having to throw your line out over sharp rocks or coral. Fishing off steep rocks works well, or if you can get beyond the reef on a raft or a canoe, you can usually catch fish just beyond the drop-off. For bait, you can use small, crushed sand crabs or shrimps which you'll find in the coral pools.

If you have a good free-diver in the group, and a mask, snorkel and fins, you will be eating well indeed. A spear gun is a great survival tool, but even without it the diver can collect crayfish and shellfish (such as conch) not available on the reef. For a diver with the gun, the seas abound with fishy meals. Remember though, that carrying bleeding fish in tropical waters may well attract sharks. Keep speared fish on a long string to be safe and get them ashore or into a boat as quickly as you can.

When the tide is out, you can hunt crabs, eels and snakes in the mud of tropical mangrove swamps. Great fun! As the tide comes in, varieties of herring and mullet can be caught either by stunning them with a paddle or beating them with a spiked stick as they gulp on the surface. You can also fish using a light line baited with a bit of crushed crab. Oysters grow on the trunks of mangroves in some parts of the tropics and are easily knocked off with a diving knife. Many birds nest in the swamp too, and you may find a nest with eggs or young. Keep an eye out for larger creatures as well. Sharks often swim right into the mangroves to feed, sometimes in as little as 2 or 3 feet of water. If you fancy shark steak, it may even be possible to lure one into an enclosed piece of the swamp with carrion or fish heads, then close his only exit and wait for him to die when the tide recedes.

Remote islands are often the nesting grounds of sea birds whose eggs can be eaten raw. So can birds themselves if the castaway is hungry and stealthy enough. Day-feeding birds may be caught sleeping on their nests at night. Night feeders, often living in burrows, may be grabbed with a gloved hand and a long arm during the day. Land crabs, lizards, snakes and wild goat are widely distributed on remote tropical islands. Turtles too may provide an excellent omelet if you can locate a new nest – identifiable from the scratchings in the sand above the high-tide mark.

If you have coconuts on your island, you have a source of food and drink, as well as material for roofing a shelter and a source of fuel. Getting any variety of food from the jungle, however, requires specific knowledge of food, plants and trees. The roots of ferns, wild taro and yams, the young centres of palms, succulent shoots of creepers and grasses, fruit and nuts, may all be found by those who know what they are looking for. If in doubt, use great caution and, to any plant which you believe may be edible, apply the following tests:

1 Are other animals (birds, pigs, insects) eating it?

2 Break it in your fingers then sniff the juice. Be suspicious of pungent juices such as are found in many lilies.

3 If the juice is not too repugnant to the nose, put a little on the tip of your tongue and leave it there for some minutes, testing it for tingling or excessively bitter warning taste.

4 Should the plant appear safe, chew a small portion, then spit it out and wait to determine the effect it has on your mouth lining.

5 Should an abundant food supply prove unpalatable raw, boil it with salt then repeat the above procedure. Many vegetable toxins are destroyed by heat.

6 No matter how tasty it seems, eat only small quantities of strange food at first.

This test is by no means infallible. Leeks, onion or garlic would probably fail, and it is possible that deadly nightshade would slip through. The best thing is obviously to know your jungle plants. Second best is to carry a manual on jungle survival to help you identify the plants you see.

Cold Weather Survival Ashore

In the event of an accident, your priorities upon reaching shore are:

1 See to the needs of anyone suffering exposure or serious injury.
2 Salvage the boat and all the equipment you can safely reach.
3 Find shelter from the elements.
4 Make a fire and dry your clothing.

If you managed to get your boat and equipment ashore, you will have the means to survive indefinitely provided you don't squander your resources.

First, build a permanent camp well protected from the wind.

Second, prepare a signal for attracting the attention of any passing vessel. A cairn with an orange survival bag over it may suit the terrain, or an SOS written in orange plastic on the rocks or snow so it can be read by aircraft. Lay a smoke fire, ready to be ignited at the sight of a vessel, and keep it dry with a sheet of plastic.

Third, all around you is food. Wilderness survival techniques can become a way of life when kayaking in the cool temperate or subarctic regions of the world, where it is usually both unnecessary and undesirable to carry masses of unpalatable freeze-dried food. All varieties of seaweed are edible. There are hundreds of edible ground plants. In season, there are wild berries rich in vitamins. There will be fish, ducks, goat, bear, deer. Water is seldom a problem in these latitudes, even on the most barren islands, since pools abound and rain is frequent.

Seals, common to most cold latitudes, can provide the

castaway with meat, oil and skins. When a colony has been located, a hunter armed only with a club can be quite successful if he approaches carefully from downwind. (You will be in no doubt as to which is downwind of one of these colonies!) The quicker you regain your hunter's instinct the better, when it comes to wilderness survival in hot or cold climes.

The French folding Nautiraid in Greenland

12
Planning an Expedition

This chapter is to help you plan a major kayak expedition either abroad or at home.

THE SCHEDULE

Most expedition schedules are governed by such considerations as the length of the favourable season and the date at which you have to be back in the city for work, but it may happen, if you take canoeing seriously, that you leave your job and put your savings into paddling some distant sea which has always fascinated you. At least I hope that is not too fantastic or improbable a suggestion.

Even with no time limit at all you still need an idea of how long your journey is going to take. You will still have to estimate costs, choose equipment, plan provisions. To do this you must estimate both the total and the average daily distance. When you divide one into the other to estimate trip time, add 20 percent for the unexpected. Most sea kayakers can easily do 20 miles a day on a short trip in good weather. Many can do 30 miles a day under such conditions, and some, like Paul Caffyn, comfortably cover 40 miles a day in a fast West Greenland-style kayak, so long as the sea is agreeable and the weather holds fair. On an expedition, however, you will not put water behind you at such speed. As a general rule,

I think in terms of 10 miles a day. For trips of less than 350 miles, the comfortable mileage may be more like 15 miles per day, whereas on a long wilderness trip, if you are surviving off the land, an average of 8 miles a day is good time. If you are exposed to continual storm, as in the Aleutian Islands, your progress could be slower still.

On an expedition, you should expect to paddle 30 or even 40 miles a day on some days, but if you plan to keep going for weeks or months, such efforts will have to be interspersed with rest days. After a 40–mile crossing, you may need three days of rest and good eating so you can maintain your strength over the long term. During a six-month trip in Chile, we evolved a routine of two days on and one day off, then two days on and two days off. This gave us one day for resting, and two days for food gathering, hunting and preparing food for the four days of travel. This is a good arrangement, but it is only possible for straightforward coastal canoeing; where you have open sea, such regular schedules have little meaning because you must keep going until you reach land.

Some kayakers, eager to spend as much time as possible in the boat, organize land-based support teams. If you have a carload of friends willing and able to follow you around and meet you most nights, as Paul Caffyn did on his circumnavigation of New Zealand, you should be able to make considerably better than 10 miles per day, since you will be able to travel more lightly (Paul usually carried only 20 lbs). You may also eat better and will probably save precious hours morning and night by not having to pitch a camp and prepare your own food. Paul averaged 21 miles a day over the two summers required for that voyage, and 26 miles a day on his well-supported voyage around the U.K. in the summer of 1980.

One of the most difficult tasks of the whole expedition is often selecting who is to go, and it is a job that has to be done right. The safest thing, one would think, should be to go with old friends – but you might in actuality be better off choosing strangers. Old friends taken out of the environment in which the friendship developed have a tendency to *become* strangers, and everyone seems to drag along unspoken preconditions and unrealistic expectations which fester badly on a long or dangerous trip. In published accounts of major expeditions, conflict is often played down, but if you read carefully you will soon realize that conflict is the rule, not the exception. Just the insecurities of being away from home, if your expedition is in foreign parts, can alter some people drastically. Add to that the element of danger and the polarizing effect of the leader and the led, and many otherwise fine friendships disintegrate in a mess of shattered personalities and failed expectations. In fact my advice – given with sadness, not cynicism – is, if you really value your friendship with someone, *don't* take him or her on a long sea kayaking expedition unless the friendship was forged on a similar trip in the first place.

I suggest you avoid taking moody and depressive people, who can badly affect group morale and may become a great liability under stress. People rigid in their ways or reluctant to chip in are no help either. (Have I just eliminated someone you know?) Be willing to judge and to trust your judgement. You will probably select the right companions intuitively and do a better job than if you psychoanalyzed everyone. All too often, though, the final decision boils down to who has the funds and the time. If you really get stuck, a carefully worded advertisement in a newspaper can produce an amusing variety of applicants from which you may well be able to select a good companion.

Before everyone makes a commitment to the trip, get your heads together and sort out what you all expect from it. This is a very important step no matter what your trip involves. Even if yours is just a bunch of friends paddling up the coast for a week, you should clarify your hopes and expectations in advance. A casual chat over a beer in the local pub may be sufficient in such a case, but if your trip has a fifty-thousand-dollar budget from a scientific foundation, forget the beer. You will have to work out in advance as much detail as you possibly can and get it down on paper – and you may also need a lawyer if the stakes are that high.

For most expeditions, however, a home-made written agreement is in order. What is needed is a statement of intent by people of good will so that in times of stress – and there are always plenty of them – the group can refer back to established common goals. The exercise of writing this statement down will serve to make quite sure you all have the same aims and priorities, and it can help in clarifying the division of workload, responsibilities and privileges as well as the financial status of the enterprise. It is usually obvious who is the expedition leader, but even if this is apparent it is sometimes a good idea also to put it down in writing.

Roles such as medic, treasurer, route researcher, secretary, photographer, equipment and insurance organizer, cinematographer, transportation officer, fund raiser and sponsor liaison officer should be allocated at this stage. If your expedition is this elaborate, the agreement should be also; and remember that it must be fair to everyone. Inequities will only fester until a more inconvenient time – such as the middle of the trip.

The agreement may cover details of finance, liabilities, distribution of profits, ownership of equipment and it may lay down procedures for resolving disputes. It should establish a policy for such occurrences as walkouts, accidents, illness and death. It can define an attitude to publicity, the acceptance of outside assistance, use of sails, hotels or tents. You should agree on a rate of travel and the relative priorities of science, filming, photography or other activities. Finally, the agreement should include a clause which spells out amendment procedures.

The Caribbean Kayak Expedition of 1977–78 was structured so all four members had a single vote, with an additional tie-breaking vote available to the leader. Since there was considerable discrepancy of experience, I was given an absolute veto on sea decisions. This, we hoped, might save us the pains of the democratic process in emergencies. I am pleased to say that at no time did I need to use either the tie-breaking vote or the veto, though we had our share of differences.

Disputes will arise. The very nature of the exercise seems to attract people with well-established personalities and strong wills. The agreement and the will to stick to it can help to resolve many of the differences. If you can preserve the willingness to discuss problems, you will be able to handle most policy and personality disputes.

PRE-DEPARTURE WORK

As D-Day draws nigh, the organizing acquires a frantic quality. Equipment piles higher and higher in various living rooms, and mountains of letters are shuffled in and out. The garbage is full of crumpled envelopes while the paperweight can hardly maintain its position on top of the ever-growing pile of exotic cancelled stamps. There is hardly a clear space to put down a cup of coffee while you answer the telephone. People are visited by gut-flutters and second thoughts as they begin to realize what they have let themselves in for. Training is well under way, muscles ache, and there is a sore spot in the place where your back rubs the backrest. The medical kit is in order and you have a memo to pick up the prohibited drugs at the airport. You have found an airline which is prepared to bend the rules and give you a discount on your air tickets and free freight in exchange for some sort of share in the glory if you succeed. Nobody has agreed to back your movie but you are still working on that.

Amid this excitement, insurance may sound a strange priority – especially from someone who has pontificated on the virtues of self-reliance – but once you have decided to travel as a group, you are obliged to take extra precautions. If you have a sponsor, you have an additional duty to keep the odds in favour of success as great as possible. Most kayak trips are run on budgets so tight that having a member hospitalized overseas could spell financial disaster for the project. It is for this reason that you need adequate insurance. I would suggest at least $5,000 medical insurance per person. Since your canoe is carrying valuable equipment, the loss of which you may not be able to absorb, you may need insurance on the goods as well.

By this time, the area you are visiting will be taking shape in your mind. You will all have read up on local history, geography and politics. You'll already have had to put plastic over your charts, not to protect them from the water, but to keep them from wearing out as you paw and ponder their mysteries. Everyone on the expedition should be familiar with the charts and see the full route mapped out on them. The leader should have them virtually memorized. Coast pilots and yachtsmen's guides should be studied carefully and marked where relevant. Escape routes should be marked for difficult passages. Where your course follows a dangerous lee shore, estimated times to safe harbour should be jotted on the chart with chinagraph pencil. Check the history of past weather from as many sources as possible and be quite sure you understand how it will affect your course. Don't hesitate to alter your plans radically as you learn more about the area you are visiting. Know what to expect from currents and winds, how frequently you can restock with food and what nature can do to supply you enroute.

You won't find room on the charts to make notations about local history and geography. Put this information into a notebook instead, where you can review it day by day as your voyage proceeds. Even if your expedition is not obligated to bring back salable photographs or publishable accounts of the wonders you encounter, you'll want for your own sake to remember to paddle up that fjord where the big glacier is hiding, or to look into that cove to see what's left of the nineteenth-century whaling station. Historical research in preparation for your expedition will not only give it an added dimension of enjoyment, it will put your effort in perspective too.

If your journey takes you through the Caribbean, along Central America or even along some of the coasts of Europe, you may face a new country and a new set of laws every few days. Again and again you may be confronted by a platoon of officials whose job is to check you out and see that your papers are in order. They may request such wonders of the past as de-ratting certificates, ship's doctor's report, quadruplicate lists of crew and cargo, as well as port clearance from the country you have just left.

Most authorities don't know how to handle the arrival of a kayak and your presence will probably be the cause of great hilarity. This can be to your advantage. While they are laughing they are unlikely to make things too difficult for you – but don't count on it.

Part of your pre-expedition work should be to contact every customs authority along your route, giving them an approximate arrival date and a list of the equipment which may be of interest to them. The letter should be addressed to the Chief Inspector of Customs and if possible should be written in the language of the country involved. They will feel better disposed towards you if you ask in advance about restricted items such as fruit and firearms. Another letter to the local diplomatic representative of each country to be visited will clear up the conflicting rumours about the various visas needed. Check to see if there are any restrictions on coastal landings or the use of cinematic equipment.

The rules vary widely. For example, if you are going to the Dominican Republic you may need a special cruising permit even to approach the shore. Some years ago, in order to cruise the remote north coast by kayak, we needed a letter from the Vice Admiral himself. (We really did need it, too. Without it we would have been explaining our position from behind bars on a number of occasions.) Often a letter from the minister of tourism will be useful as well, but in troubled areas nothing may help. Charles Miller, an American canoeist who has paddled extensively in the Aegean and Greek Islands, tells of intensive interrogations by both Greek and Turkish authorities, and reports that both Bulgarian and Rumanian shore patrols fired shots at him.

In more volatile countries, your embassy should be given your schedule and contacted as regularly as they advise. If you present your passport to them on your day of arrival, you may have an easier time replacing it should it be lost. Where political unrest is extreme, notify all local authorities whenever you arrive in a town. (You may have to do this anyway.) Remember that after a few days' paddling, a canoeist can look as wild and woolly as any guerrilla or desperado, and jumpy authorities may need a little reassurance. A good trick is to contact the local press as soon as you get to the country where you plan to paddle. You can give them a photograph of you in your boats and an outline of the trip, then keep several copies of the published article. When you are later faced with a suspicious police officer or a gibbering soldier with a machine gun, you can wave your press clipping at him; it is an impressive example of the power of the printed word.

My first Patagonian kayak trip began only three months after the overthrow of Allende, at a time when the military were still pulling communists out from under the beds. Near the end of the six-month trip, the police picked me up while I was taking photographs in the poor part of the town of Castro, on the Island of Chiloe. I did look suspicious (though I was not under my bed). I was wearing a bushy beard, beret, and I had a military-looking pack full of fancy cameras. I had loose ammunition in my pockets and my visa had expired, yet none of this mattered once I produced the newspaper clippings with the story of our expedition. To my considerable relief, I was immediately treated as a bosom friend and a special letter was provided to cover the expired visa which could only be renewed in Santiago.

There is, of course, another way to do things if your party is really small and you make absolutely no contact with the press – and *if* the countries you visit are safe and peaceful. During my first paddle through the Caribbean, in 1967, I was so ignorant of procedure that I entered and left half a dozen countries without bothering to disturb the authorities at all. Nobody complained. I just paddled up to a white sandy beach, made my camp, caught my fish, bought my stores in the local town and moved on. People who saw me thought I had come from one of the cruise yachts or from the next town. Nobody suspected I had paddled in from the faded blue island on the horizon. I do not seriously advocate this procedure, however, since it *could* get you into trouble and spoil your trip. There is usually little to be gained from it anyway, since most authorities are friendly to kayakers.

One of your most important pre-departure contacts is the coast guard. Write and tell them your plan before you get where you're going. Once you arrive, contact them personally and discuss with them, in as much detail as they can bear, the finer points of your journey through their jurisdiction. Give them an outline of your schedule – but with a reasonable delay factor, in case you are holed up on a beach during bad weather. You can do without the embarrassment of an unnecessary rescue. Let the coast guard know your storm procedure so they can anticipate your thinking in case there *is* a need to search.

It can save time if you carry a printed list of expedition information useful to coast guard and other local authorities. As well as your route, it should contain a description of your boats and the names, addresses and next of kin of all members. List the safety equipment you carry, as well as your expected supply of water and food. If you carry a radar reflector, tell them that.

The attitudes of coast guards vary more from station to station than nation to nation. Generally, though, you will find them friendly, helpful and prone to underestimate kayaks. One blustery Easter day when we contacted the British coast guard at Dover to tell them we were paddling to Calais, they not only gave us detailed advice on currents and weather but also actually drove us about in search of some last-minute safety equipment we had been unable to pick up in London. Miami coast guard were just the opposite. When we contacted them from the Bahamas to warn of our attempt at the treacherous 62–mile crossing of the Gulf Stream, they did not want to know. "If you aren't in trouble, we don't want to hear from you," their operator said curtly, and then hung up. They did not even record the frequency of our radio transmitter – a simple enough precaution which could have saved them a lot of effort, not to mention our lives. (Miami is a busy shipping area, of course, but Dover Strait is busier.) Fortunately, the Miami experience is not typical. The U.S.

coast guard in Puerto Rico was extremely helpful that trip, and we were able to return the favour by assisting in the prosecution of an oil tanker we photographed pumping its bilges between the islands.

SPONSORS

Most sea kayaking expeditions are financed entirely by the members, but lengthy ones in foreign waters can be too expensive for ordinary folk. You somehow have to find enough money for boats, equipment, food, transport, freight, medical and equipment insurance, cameras, film, spending money and a 20 percent contingency fund. When costs are high, finding a sponsor may be your only hope.

Promotional exercises can actually be arranged with little disruption of the expedition and a minimum of embarrassment, since the advertising work will all be done by your backer's ad agency. Such an arrangement can save you thousands of dollars and greatly enhance your expedition's chances of success.

The important thing to remember when seeking a sponsor is that they too will want something out of the deal. Begging letters only cause irritation and waste postage. Instead, think carefully about which manufacturer could use your trip to promote its product, then write the company a letter outlining the trip and the ways you would be prepared to assist with promotions in return for assistance. You should include a detailed outline of your track record – previous expeditions and any satisfied sponsors you may have had in the past – and a profile of each crew member. If your list does not look very impressive, you will have to produce a very good

idea for the actual kayak trip and promote your cause personally. It can be a disheartening business. Even when you are
sure a company could benefit from your trip, you may have no
joy convincing their advertising manager and will probably
have the greatest difficulty just getting to see him. Make your
plans at least a year in advance to avoid being told that "this
year's advertising budget has been fully allocated."

Lay hands on all the newspapers of the area into which you
plan to paddle (the country's embassy will have them) and read
the advertisements. Find out who is spending money on newspaper advertising and what angle they are using, then tailor
your proposal accordingly. But be warned: few advertising
managers have the imagination or nerve to risk a break with
tradition. You might point out to your potential backer – and
to yourself – that Columbus, Magellan, Vasco da Gama and
Marco Polo were all sponsored by commercial interests. Still,
it is likely to be an uphill job.

If yours is a noteworthy adventure, you can get assistance
from newspapers and magazines themselves, but make sure
you don't give away more than they are paying for. Here you
will need a very knowledgeable friend ashore, or a professional
agent. But take care. Publicity, far more than commercial
sponsorship and promotion, can seriously warp the adventure
itself.

PHYSICAL PREPARATION

Sea kayaking depends on stamina and efficiency more than
strength, and stamina, apart from being a mental attitude,
depends on training and being fit. Set your body a tough
training schedule including regular sessions in the boats and
general fitness activities such as running, swimming and
exercises for the back and arms.

An excellent specialized exercise, which can be done before going to bed each night, requires an 18-inch stick and a good hefty climbing boot. Tie the boot to the centre of the stick with a 5-foot bootlace. Hold the arms out horizontally and wind the boot up the stick, then wind it steadily down again. Start with five of these exercises, then increase by one every night until you are doing thirty. This is a fine exercise for arms and shoulders and you will have the chance to explore the subtle distinction between stoicism and masochism without even having to get into a kayak. As for the kayaking side of the training, get out there and train hard in the boats at every opportunity. Most kayaking discomfort results from sitting in one position for long periods of time, and from chafing. There seems to be no way to improve one's tolerance to these evils, but do take the trouble to rig yourself a comfortable seat. The only training for endurance is to endure – and that, I am afraid, is what sitting on your butt for twelve hours is all about.

If your expedition takes you to a new climatic zone, you will need to allow a period for adjustment to the new conditions. Two weeks at least will be needed when travelling to the tropics from a temperate climate. Ease up your training program a little when you get there and take care to drink plenty of water and take extra salt. Moving to colder climates, you will have to make a conscious effort to underdress. Cold swims will help with this adjustment.

EXPEDITIONARY PHOTOGRAPHIC EQUIPMENT

Photography is an important aspect of most kayak expeditions, both for personal interest and as a means of recouping some costs. First class photographs can be salable in themselves and are usually essential for selling magazine articles and illustrating lectures. A commercial photographer is a good person to have on any trip and it is useful if every member is armed with a camera as well.

The SLR 35 mm is undoubtedly the most favoured expedition camera since it is compact, sophisticated and robust with a wide selection of lenses available for the major brand names. Nikon, Leica, Pentax, Canon and Olympus are all well-established brands suitable for expedition work, but best of all is the Nikonos waterproof camera. The 35 mm lens with which it is normally equipped is of fine quality and does not have so wide an angle as to distort the image significantly for middle distance pictures. The camera can also take an 80 mm lens and, if you are feeling rich, a 15 mm one. Maintenance is simple. You have only to keep the O-rings greased and free of grit and give it the occasional scrub with fresh water and a toothbrush. The camera can safely be left slopping around in water at the bottom of your canoe all day. The only place you cannot carry the Nikonos is in direct sunlight, since the heat will ruin the film.

An ordinary SLR camera must be protected inside a waterproof container. Klepper's tough, rubberized canvas clothes bag with a fold-up entrance is reliable for keeping cameras dry if sufficient care is taken in closing it. The bag has a separate inflatable compartment to give added buoyancy. I keep my own cameras in a homemade fibreglass box, reinforced with steel and topped with a fold-down lid which pressure-seals against an O-ring of silicone rubber. This has successfully protected them through two capsizes (once floating for 45 minutes) and many miles of sea kayaking during the past ten years. The box, which is strong enough for a heavy man to stand on, is built to fit into an old army '44 pack which effectively disguises its contents. It neatly fits my kayak.

EXPEDITIONS OF NOVICES

Many outdoor centres and even regular schools have fine programs which involve ocean kayaking. Here, an entirely different approach is needed from the one I have stressed in this book. I have preached self-reliance and total acceptance of responsibility for one's actions. But the organizer of an expedition of novices must be a defensive thinker – defensive to the point of extreme caution.

If your group includes individuals in the 13 to 16 age group (a child any younger should be in a double with an experienced adult), take special precautions against hypothermia, since children can succumb much more quickly than adults. If possible, wetsuits should be worn, and warm, windproof clothing kept handy.

The organizer of juvenile groups would be wise to *personally* see to it that every boat has the required safety equipment and that everyone – including instructors – wears a life jacket and has a windproof anorak.

Often, novice parties are too large and unwieldy. If you decide to send young novices to sea in kayaks, you are, in my view, obligated to provide massive supervision by experienced adults. I believe that open-sea kayak excursions for juveniles with an experienced-to-inexperienced ratio greater than 1:2 should have a safety boat. The question to ask yourself is, can you as leader handle an emergency when all the novices are in trouble at the same time? *You cannot afford to run novice trips if the answer to that question is no.*

I was once with a group of Outward Bound boys on a sea trip in New Zealand's Marlborough Sounds. There were fourteen boys, 16 to 19 years old, in slalom singles making a 2–mile crossing of a bay during rough weather. A savage squall capsized nine of them in one blast. It was so rough that any form of group rescue using the techniques they had been taught was out of the question (even though they had unloaded canoes). There were two instructors with the group and myself and another instructor shadowing them in a 24-foot jet rescue boat, watching through binoculars from a distance of a half mile. We had picked up all nine canoeists and their boats in less than twenty minutes. Without the rescue boat, we would have needed a 1:1 staff-to-pupil ratio to handle the emergency, and even then the result would have been in doubt. A host of errors can be glossed over by having a good safety boat. I hold no brief for safety boats on expeditions of experienced sea kayakers, where the boat would extinguish much of the point of sea kayaking, but if you are running a novice expedition, take a safety boat whenever you have any doubts.

Appendix:
A Transatlantic Solo

On the morning of 1 August 1928, Capt. Franz Romer was discovered fast asleep in his kayak in the harbour of St. Thomas, Virgin Islands. Romer had paddled and sailed nearly 4000 miles from Lisbon, Portugal, via Las Palmas in the Canary Islands. He had encountered two hurricanes – one between Lisbon and Las Palmas, and another between Las Palmas and St. Thomas – and on the last leg of his journey had been continuously at sea for two months. Between April and August the New York Times *carried several brief articles on Romer's voyage. A more extensive report appeared in the issue for Sunday, 23 September 1928 – ten days after it was written. Here are some excerpts.*

SAN JUAN, PORTO RICO, Sept. 13 – ... Captain Romer's visit here was unheralded. He put into port from St. Thomas after about twenty hours' sailing time. At St. Thomas he had had a rest of six weeks after 58 days of calm and storm from Las Palmas, Canary Islands, to the Virgin Islands. His experiences during that time can best be imagined, for he spoke little of them. He knew though, he said, that he was going to get all the way across the Atlantic, and he still had the greatest confidence in reaching the United States safely when he left here. From Florida he plans to make his way up the coast to New York City. If possible he will fly back to Germany. Neither the air nor the sea nor things above or beneath seem to have any terrors for him.

Other men have crossed the Atlantic alone in various kinds

of boats, have gone around the world, in fact. But Captain Romer's craft is certainly the first of its kind to venture on such a journey and probably the tiniest.

The *Deutscher Sport* is a wooden frame craft of the sailing canoe type, covered with rubber and canvas. It is 21 feet long with [2.5] feet of beam, and a depth from canvas covered deck to rubber bottom of 18 inches. Frame and covering may be dismounted and rolled in a bundle a man might haul under his arm. It carries an 8–foot mast. The deck is not more than 6 inches above the water line. At most times it is awash. So close is Romer to the water all the time that he may drop his hands over the sides and dabble in the ocean. Water is kept out of the cockpit by means of rubber sheets which he fastens to a framework about the cockpit and then about himself. At night he may cover himself over completely with a combination helmet and cape of rubber which he fastens to the deck. He then breathes through a tube, gas-mask fashion. He puts this on instead of pajamas when he goes to bed – and going to bed is just the same as sitting up. His navigating instruments include a small compass, barometer, sextant and glasses. At St. Thomas, Captain Romer mounted a small out-board motor that was sent out from Germany. He said the motor might come in handy in the case he ran into hurricane weather. His fuel supply – five gallons – was lashed on deck just aft of the tiny cockpit.

The craft is Captain Romer's own design and he set sail in it from Lisbon, Portugal, on the last day of March....

What happened during those first days of the lonely voyage only Captain Romer and his log know. Some day he may publish his log. He told little here. But he suggested enough to set the imagination to work. For instance, he said that the seas were so high at times that he did not even think whether he would ride them. When he anchored at Las Palmas he said he knew that his trip would be successful, that nothing any worse than the experiences of the first part of his journey could possibly befall him.

In those first days there were periods when he was wholly unconscious, he believes, and other times when he was only partly conscious. He managed to keep his course much of the time with rudder line tied to the boom so that it mattered little whether he was asleep or awake. But there were days and nights when he had no sleep. And during all this time he was steeling himself to the discomfort and soreness that came from the necessity to remain for hours in one position; the exposure to sun and wind and rain and spray; fair days and storm; nights of either stars or clouds. And day or night for companions he had the waves and the uncommunicative inhabitants of the sea. Sometimes he sang to all outdoors, or talked to himself.

Arriving at Las Palmas on April 17, it was not until June 2 that he got underway again. During that time he says he was ill and had a fever. If it was from exhaustion he neither admitted nor suggested it. But during that six weeks he got himself in shape to sail again, only to find that officials were so astounded at his daring that they refused him clearance papers for his ship. He slipped out of port at night.

If it may be said he had a little more room in his canoe after leaving Las Palmas it is as much figure of speech as fact. At Lisbon he had stored in almost the entire hold of his craft sufficient supplies of food and water to last him across the Atlantic. The more food and water there was, the less room he had to stretch his legs. Gradually he ate himself into his own ship....

From Las Palmas Captain Romer set out again, little dreaming that it would take him 58 days to travel the 2,730 miles between Las Palmas and St. Thomas. At St. Thomas they gave him an official public reception and a medal. But this was after he had caught a few winks of sleep and visited the barber for the first time in two months and had had a chance to park his canoe in George Levi's store, where thousands viewed it with much awe and exclamation.

Between Las Palmas and St. Thomas there were days of dead calm, days of blistering heat, days and nights of storm. Sun and salt spray tortured Romer's hands and arms, and they were swollen and blistered and stiff. He lost his hat in a wind. Then his head and neck and back got more of the sun. He sat until he could sit no more. He stood until his feet and legs would bear his weight no longer. Then he sat some more. Three sharks took a curious fancy to his craft. They played about the canoe, swimming from side to side, at times darting under the boat and coming so close that he could feel the scrape of the fins through the flexible rubber bottom. Romer, lonely, talked to the sharks. They swam away.

His trip from St. Thomas to San Juan was probably the shortest leg of his whole trip to New York, unless he makes more stops up the coast than he seemed to have in mind here.

Romer is 29 and was born at Constance, in South Germany.... During the war he was in submarines, and before that he worked in the Zeppelin plant. After the war, for a time, he took up aviation and later went to sea.

Captain Romer said he did not swim. "What good would it do me?" he asked.

A few days after the foregoing piece was written and before it was published, Romer slipped out of San Juan harbour, missing the hurricane warning which apparently had just been posted. The addition of motor and fuel tank had ruined the trim of his kayak, but given the fierceness of the storm he unwittingly paddled into – surely the worst of the three he met on that voyage – it is hard to believe that he would have survived even in a perfectly balanced craft. As it is, no one ever saw Franz Romer or his boat again.

Bibliography

This list includes many but by no means all of the existing English-language publications about sea kayaks and sea kayaking, as well as a select few of the basic reference works useful to any expeditionary sea canoeist. Coast pilots, pilot guides and sailing directions for individual areas, though vitally important, are quite numerous and are therefore omitted from the list. Generally speaking, the most useful pilot guides and coast pilots are those published by the National Ocean Survey or the Defense Mapping Agency Hydrographic Center in the United States, and by the British Admiralty in the U.K. For Canadian waters, excellent sailing directions are published by the Canadian Department of Fisheries and Oceans. Several Scandinavian countries publish good pilot guides to their own coasts, and the Danish government also publishes a pilot guide which is particularly useful for Greenland waters.

Admiralty Manual of Navigation. London: H.M. Stationery Office. 1970.

ADNEY, EDWIN, & CHAPELLE, HOWARD. *The Bark Canoes and Skin Boats of North America.* Washington, D.C.: Smithsonian Institution. 1964.

BASCOM, WILLARD. *Waves and Beaches.* Garden City, N.Y.: Anchor. 1964.

BOWDITCH, NATHANIEL, et al. *American Practical Navigator.* Washington, D.C.: Defense Mapping Agency Hydrographic Center. Rev. ed. 1977.

BROWER, KENNETH. *The Starship and the Canoe*. New York: Holt, Rinehart. 1973.

CAFFYN, PAUL. *Obscured by Waves*. Dunedin, N.Z.: John McIndoe. 1979.

COCK, OLIVER J. *A Short History of Canoeing in Britain*. London: British Canoeing Union. 1974.

DURHAM, BILL. *Canoes and Kayaks of Western America*. Seattle: Copper Canoe Press. 1960.

[DUTTON, BENJAMIN] *Dutton's Navigation & Piloting*. 13th rev. ed. by Elbert S. Maloney. Annapolis, Md.: Naval Institute Press. 1978.

FENGER, FREDERIC ABILDGAARD. *Alone in the Caribbean*. Belmont, Mass.: Wellington Books. 1958.

FERRERO, FRANCO, & HAIRON, DEREK. *Jersey Canoe Club Circumnavigation of Ireland, 1978*. n.p. [Jersey, Channel Is.] n.d. [mimeographed booklet, 60 pp]

FURSE, CHRIS. *Elephant Island: An Antarctic Expedition*. Shrewsbury, Shrops.: Anthony Nelson. 1979.

GOODMAN, FRANK R., ed. *British Kayak Expedition Cape Horn: Official Expedition Report*. n.p. [Nottingham, Notts.] n.d. [1978] [printed pamphlet, 24 pp]

HARRISON, MARK, et al. *Circumnavigation of Ireland by Kayak Expedition, 1978*. Durham: College of St. Hild & St. Bede. n.d. [booklet, 42 pp]

HAYWARD, J.S., et al. *Survival Suits for Accidental Immersion in Cold Water: Design-Concepts* [sic] *and their Thermal Protection Performance*. Victoria, B.C.: University of Victoria, Dept. of Biology. 1978.

HUTCHINSON, DEREK C. *Sea Canoeing*. London: A. & C. Black. 1976. [includes useful bibliography]

KEMP, JOHN F., ed. *Reed's Ocean Navigator*. London: Thomas Reed. 3rd ed. 1977.

KNIGHT, AUSTIN MELVIN. *Knight's Modern Seamanship.* New York: Van Nostrand. 1977.

LINDEMANN, HANNES. *Alone at Sea.* New York: Random House. 1958. [German original: *Allein über den Ozean.* Frankfurt am Main: Scheffler. 1957.]

MC KIE, RONALD CECIL HAMLYN. *The Heroes.* New York: Harcourt. 1960.

MORTLOCK, COLIN, & SMITH, BARRY. *The British Pacific-Alaskan Kayak Expedition, 1979.* n.p. [Dunfermline, Fife?] n.d. [1979] [booklet]

MUENCH-KHE, WILLI. *Kapitän Romer bezwingt den Atlantik: ein Tatsachenbericht.* Potsdam: Zeltbücherei. 1939.

Nautical Almanac. Washington, D.C.: U.S. Naval Observatory, & London: H.M. Stationery Office. Issued annually.

PHILLIPS, CECIL ERNEST LUCAS. *Cockleshell Heroes.* London: Heinemann. 1957.

RAMWELL, J.J. *Sea Touring.* Huntingdon, Cambs.: John J. Ramwell. 1976.

Report of the 1977 North Wales Kayak Expedition to North West Greenland. n.p. [North Wales] n.d. [booklet, 54 pp]

Report of the Sea Touring Symposium, Newman College, Birmingham, 18th & 19th December 1977. n.p. [Birmingham, W. Midlands] n.d. [1978] [mimeographed pamphlet, 20 + 4 pp]

ROBERTSON, DOUGAL. *Sea Survival.* London: Elek. 1975.

ROBERTSON, DOUGAL. *Survive the Savage Sea.* London: Elek. 1973.

SHUFELDT, H.H., & DUNLOP, G.D. *Piloting and Dead Reckoning.* Annapolis, Md.: Naval Institute Press. 1970.

TRICKER, R.A.R. *Bores, Breakers, Waves and Wakes.* London: Mills & Boon. 1964.

WATTS, ALAN. *Weather Forecasting Ashore and Afloat.* London: Adlard Coles. 1968.

WATTS, ALAN. *Wind Pilot.* Lymington, Hants.: Nautical Publishing. 1975.

WILKERSON, JAMES A., ed. *Medicine for Mountaineering.* Seattle: The Mountaineers. 1967.

ZIMMERLY, DAVID W. "An Illustrated Glossary of Kayak Terminology." *Canadian Museums Association Gazette* 9, (1976): 27–37.

Index